THE COMPLETE
CHINESE CRESTED

BRENDA JONES

RINGPRESS

THIS BOOK IS DEDICATED TO
STAROUND TYLA,
THE CHINESE CRESTED
RESPONSIBLE FOR DRAWING
MY ATTENTION TO
THIS DELIGHTFUL BREED
SO MANY YEARS AGO.

Ringpress Books, PO Box 8, Lydney,
Gloucestershire GL15 6YD, United Kingdom.
ISBN 0 948955 46 5

Printed in Singapore.

ACKNOWLEDGEMENTS

Amy Fernandez (USA), the late John
Curvengen, Carl Lindemeaier and Diane
Pearce for photographs, not forgetting
my husband Barrie for all his
encouragement.

CONTENTS

Introduction   7
Chapter One: Origins   9
Chapter Two: The Xoloitzcuintli   15
Chapter Three: The Chinese Crested   27
Chapter Four: The Genetics of Hairlessness   39
Chapter Five: Dentition   45
Chapter Six: The British Breed Standard   49
Chapter Seven: The Chinese Crested in America   63
Chapter Eight: Breeding   75
Chapter Nine: Whelping and Weaning   79
Chapter Ten: Selecting and Caring for a Puppy   89
Chapter Eleven: Care of the Adult Chinese Crested   95
Chapter Twelve: Digestion   101
Chapter Thirteen: In the Show Ring   106
Chapter Fourteen: Judging   110
Chapter Fifteen: The Future   113
Chapter Sixteen: Best of the Foundation Stock   117
Chapter Seventeen: The Champions – British   124
                                              – American   149
Appendix: Breed Clubs   159

INTRODUCTION

Since the Chinese Crested was reintroduced into Great Britain in 1965, interest in the breed has grown steadily. Careful breeding and the increased knowledge of the genetics of hairlessness, has brought about a marked improvement in the quality and soundness of these highly intelligent, delightful little dogs. A small core of breeders are determined to continue the longterm dedication required to improve and conserve this ancient breed.

Luckily the Chinese Crested is not a commercial breed, and those who try to exploit it purely for money soon find it does not pay dividends. If you want the challenge of competing in the show ring, and attempting to breed a team of outstanding dogs, this is the breed for you. Alternatively, if it is just a pet that you want, you will be rewarded with the affection and devotion of a very special and unusual dog. Chinese Crested make ideal companions and are excellent watch dogs; they are not particularly yappy, but a group will howl occasionally. People who suffer from asthma may find that they can live with a hairless Chinese Crested, when they are unable to tolerate a coated dog.

This book has been written purely with the Chinese Crested and its particular needs in mind. There are many excellent specialist books available on breeding and rearing dogs, and I am not attempting to cover these areas in the same depth. The chapters which follow are intended for novice and experienced dog owners, who have just discovered this fascinating breed.

*Pre-Columbian
pottery dog.*

Chapter One

ORIGINS

The origin of the hairless breeds of dog of the world is steeped in myths and legends. It is thought that the numerous hairless breeds originated in Africa, hence its genus Canis Africanus. They have survived through the centuries and are found in many sub-tropical locations throughout the world. They have been located in Mexico, China, Turkey, Peru, Ethiopia, Paraguay, Argentina, the Caribbean and the Philippines.

Archaeological evidence has shown that a small hairless dog lived in Mexico for thousands of years. When tombs in ancient burial sites have been excavated, skeletons and clay figures of hairless dogs have been found. The dog was held in great reverence during the Toltec period of 900-1200 AD. It was classed as one of the ten symbols of good, belonging to the Kingdom of the god Quetzalcoatl, the all-good. The dog represented love. The ancient Toltecs thought a dog's love for its master was the most perfect manifestation of unselfish love. When the master died, his dog was buried in the same grave. According to legend, the spirit of the dog followed its master, and when he had to account for all his good and evil deeds, the dog testified in his favour. The dog was the only possession taken

Engraving taken from a very old reference book, accompanied by the following text: "The only remaining of a litter of six, born from parents imported from China, both of which are now dead. She is two years old (1866) but has never bred in consequence of a difficulty in finding a mate of the same strain. As would be expected from her greyhound shape, she is fast and active, very affectionate in disposition, so that if the breed could be naturalised it would be acceptable to many as a novelty in the pet department. Thanks to the late Dorothy Tyler.

African Hairless dogs: Ting of Helouan and Minnie of Mincah.

Thomas Fall.

The Chinese Crested, dated 1935.

to the other world. The Aztecs later conquered the Toltecs and the spiritual image of the dog was destroyed. It was eaten as sacred food at festivals. Hairless dogs were also thought to have medicinal properties, giving relief from asthma, as well as from other aches and pains. They were also used as body-warmers. No one knows when the first hairless dogs arrived in China. They were certainly bred during the Han Dynasty, and in the 16th century Chinese merchants took them to a number of different countries.

The Chinese Crested is often confused with the Mexican Hairless – and vice versa. In fact there are a number of hairless breeds including the larger Xoloitzcuintli, the Inca Orchid, the Abyssinian Sand Dog, the Turkish Greyhound, the African Elephant Dog and the Indian Rampur Dog. The *Book Of The Dog,* which dates from the early 1900s, also mentions hairless dogs that have been found in Central and South America, West Indies, China, the Philippines and parts of Africa. It describes a very large racy type and a shorter, less elegant type. Their weight varied from four to five pounds, and from ten to fifteen pounds. Their dentition was also described as being abnormal. There is further evidence of a hairless breed in a painting by the 15th century artist Gerard David. The picture entitled *Christ Nailed To The Cross* clearly shows a little hairless dog with an excellent crest, socks, and a plume on its tail.

As with the Chinese Crested, the exact origin of the Mexican Hairless and the larger Xoloitzcuintli disappears through the centuries. It is said that they accompanied the Indians in the migration from Asia to Alaska across the Bering Strait. They are mentioned in all Pre-Columbian histories, engravings and legends.

A small statue of a woman embracing a Xoloitzcuintli has been discovered by archaeologists, and it is believed to be 3400 years years old. Many ceramic hairless dogs have been found in the Colima territory of Western Mexico, which is many hundreds of miles from Aztec territory, proving that hairless dogs were widely distributed. The explorer Francisco Hernandez, who lived in Mexico in the 1500s, was the first to describe the dogs of the country. He described the Mexican Hairless as being fairly large, about three feet long in body, with slate-coloured skin and no hair. The dogs were wrapped in cloth at night to protect them from the cold. If all these historical descriptions are correct, then the Mexican Hairless is one of the oldest unchanged breeds in America.

*A Standard
Xoloitzcuintli.*

Chapter Two

THE XOLOITZCUINTLI

The most well-known hairless breeds that are exhibited are the Chinese Crested, Mexican Hairless and the larger Xoloitzcuintli. In Great Britain it is only the Chinese Crested that is exhibited, although from time to time one or two Xoloitzcuintlis and Mexican Hairless have been imported. It is therefore curious that the breeds should be confused when they have most probably never been seen by the general public.

All hairless breeds have two varieties. Those without hair on their bodies – Hairless, and those fully-coated – referred to as Powderpuffs. The unique difference between the Chinese Crested and other hairless breeds is that the Chinese Crested carries the gene for long hair. All the others have a short coat. In the hairless varieties the hair appears on the head, feet and tail, referred to as crest, socks and plume. The Xoloitzcuintli (pronounced show-lo-eets-quintli) come in a wide range of sizes from toy to standard. The toy, which is known as the Mexican Hairless, can vary from three pounds in weight and seven inches in height to twelve pounds and up to thirteen inches. Miniatures range from fourteen to eighteen inches and weigh approximately fifteen pounds. The standard Xoloitzcuintli will be at least eighteen inches in height and can be as tall as twenty-five inches, weighing between forty and seventy-five pounds.

THE HISTORY OF THE XOLOITZCUINTLI

The history of the Xolo predates any historical reference to the Chinese Crested by more than 2000 years. It is one of the world's oldest and rarest breeds, and can justly be called the first dog of the Americas. Archaeological evidence indicates that Xolos accompanied man on his first migrations across the Bering Straits. They were highly prized for their curative and mystical powers, and as a result the breed's purity has been maintained throughout the ages. Ancient clay representations show that the Xolo has remained virtually unchanged for centuries and modern-day Xolos bear a striking resemblance to these primeval artifacts.

The name Xoloitzcuintli is derived from the name of the Aztec Indian god Xolotl and 'itzcuintli' – the Aztec word for dog. The Xolo had special religious significance for many ancient cultures. Clay and ceramic effigies of Xolos date back over 3000 years and have been discovered in the tombs of the Toltec, Aztec, Mayan, Zapoteca and Colima Indians. The famous pottery dogs of Colima provide evidence of the intricate bond which has existed between man and Xolo for centuries.

The Xolo's reputation as a healer persists to this day. The dog is believed to ward off and cure numerous ailments including rheumatism, asthma, toothache and insomnia, and there are remote villages in Mexico and Central America where Xolos are still kept specifically for their healing powers. It is impossible to quantify their effectiveness in this area, but undoubtedly the gentle warmth of the Xolo skin does have a palliative effect on the sufferer.

The breed has always been esteemed as guards and protectors, and Xolos were believed to safeguard the home from evil spirits as well as intruders. In ancient times Xolos were often sacrificed and buried with their masters in order to guide the soul on its journey to the underworld. Xolos were also used as a food source throughout Mexico and Central America. Many believed that eating the meat of a Xolo would offer a form of spiritual protection. Dogs were considered a great delicacy and consumed for sacrificial rites, marriage celebrations and funerals. There were special meanings attached to the different colours of Xolos, and so specific dogs were chosen to match the ritual or ceremony.

RECOGNITION AND REGISTRATION OF XOLOS

Xolos first came to the attention of the American Kennel Club in 1887. At that time Toy Xolos (then known as Mexican Hairless) were fully recognized by the A.K.C. and the first dogs to be registered were from Mexican stock. But the breed was so rare and was exhibited so infrequently that it was dropped by the A.K.C. in 1959. Fortunately, the Canadian Kennel Club did not follow this course and in 1989 the first Toy Xolo was made up to become a Canadian Champion.

Miniature and Standard Xolos were first registered in Mexico in 1955. Before then the breed was kept alive by secluded Indian tribes in remote parts of Mexico and Central America. Countess Lascelles de Premio Real is primarily responsible for re-establishing this almost extinct native breed. She launched a rescue campaign to find dogs and introduce them into organized breeding programmes She has since bred over twenty Xolo litters and the breed is now designated as the official dog of Mexico. There is an internationally accepted standard for Xolos and they are recognized by the Federation Cynologique Internationale based in Belgium. Xolos are often exhibited at dog shows throughout Europe and South America.

CHARACTERISTICS OF THE BREED

The distinctive prehistoric looks of the Xolo, and the choice of three sizes, make this breed a joy to own, particularly as it is such an easy breed to care for. It also has the advantage of being hypoallergenic and can usually be tolerated by allergy sufferers. With their aristocratic bearing and sleek outline, Xolos are often compared to Dobermans or Manchester Terriers. They are just as sturdy and fearless as their larger counterparts, and the name Toy

*A Hairless Toy
Xoloitzcuintli:
Razzmatazz
Neptuna.*

*A Coated Toy
Xoloitzcuintli:
Razzmatazz
Lapwing.*

belies the truth. All three sizes exhibit the typical temperament of a working breed. They are reserved and wary of strangers, but they are neither timid nor aggressive. Although patient with children and other pets, Xolos do not happily tolerate an outsider in their home. Their reputation as guard dogs is well deserved. A Xolo is extremely affectionate with its owner, but it is not demonstrative with others. The Xolo is quick to develop an undying devotion to one person, and often pines away in their master's absence. As a breed they are remarkably easy to house-train. They are fastidious in their personal habits and will even clean and groom themselves like a cat.

There are two varieties of Xolos – Hairless and Coated. The Hairless variety have a short tuft of hair on their head, tail and feet. Their skin is thick and protective, and is highly resistant to injury, sunburn and insects. Yet it feels soft, smooth and warm to the touch. The coated variety is covered in a short, smooth, dense coat. Darker colours predominate: black, slate and blue, but lighter shades of liver, bronze and red are also seen. Most Xolos are of a solid colour and many have small white markings on the chest. Brindle, spotted and black-and-tan dogs are rarer, but they do occur.

BREED STANDARD FOR THE XOLOITZCUINTLI

GENERAL APPEARANCE: A dog of clean and graceful outline, combining the elegance of a sight hound with the strength and proportion of a terrier. Noble demeanor.

HEAD: Similar to a wedge, never coarse or snipey. Muzzle somewhat longer than cranium. Stop not very pronounced. Jawline blends smoothly with base of muzzle. Nose should be in keeping with the color of the dog. Lips perfectly covering the teeth.

TEETH: Scissor or level bite. Absence of all premolars is not to be penalised in the hairless variety. Full dentition required in the coated variety.

EYES: Almond-shaped, of medium size; neither sunken nor

protruding. The color should be in keeping with the color of the dog. Both eyes must be the same color.

EARS: Large and expressive, with a thin, delicate texture. Inserted laterally and carried erect when alert.

EXPRESSION: Thoughtful and intelligent; will show distinctive brow wrinkles when at attention.

NECK AND SHOULDERS: Neck long and slightly arched, widening gracefully into sloping shoulders.

BODY: Somewhat longer than height in a 9:10 ratio. back firm, broad and well-muscled. Backline practically level from shoulder to loin, slight arch over loin. Croup rounded and very slightly sloping. Belly well tucked up. Brisket welll developed to the point of the elbow. Ribs well sprung, but not barrel-shaped. Forequarters should convey strength without any suggestion of a bulldog appearance.

LEGS: Forelegs are straight and parallel when viewed from all sides, set well under body. Well-proportioned and of sufficient length to permit a long and elegant stride. Strong pasterns and good bone. Powerful hindquarters. Hocks well let down, straight and parallel. Angulation sufficient for a full, free driving action in balance with the forequarters.

FEET: Hare foot, webbed, well-arched toes. Dewclaws may be removed.

TAIL: Set low, long and fine, reaching to the hock. Carried gaily, but not over back.

GAIT: Smooth and free-moving trot, commensurate with the size of the dog.

SKIN: Smooth, soft and warm. Small amount of coarse hair permitted only on forehead, toes and tip of tail.

COAT: Short, flat and dense. No thin or bare patches.

COLOR: All colors allowable – solid, marked or splashed.

TEMPERAMENT: Dignified, gentle and calm. Reserved with strangers but never timid or aggressive. Correct temperament is an outstanding feature of this breed; its importance cannot be over-emphasised.

HEIGHT:
Standard 18ins. to 22.5ins. Working Group
Miniature: 13ins. to 18ins. Non-Sporting Group
Toy: Under 13ins. Toy Group

Reproduced by kind permission of the American Kennel Club.

GENERAL CARE

In common with many hairless breeds, Xolos are often lacking their premolars and exhibit forward-pointing canine teeth, similar to tusks. This is not the case with the coated variety which has normal dentition.

Although they feel quite warm to the touch, the body temperature of a Xolo is the same as any other breed. The sensation of warmth is due to the lack of insulating hair-coat. Xolos are a hardy breed and do not require much special care. They do feel the cold and appreciate a sweater or blanket. The skin will benefit from an occasional rubbing with oil or lotion, and they should be bathed weekly to prevent pimples and blackheads.

An occasional currying will maintain the smart appearance of the Coated variety. Xolos do well on any high quality commercial diet, and they are especially fond of fruit and vegetables. The breed appears to have a high natural resistance to fleas, ticks and many common canine illnesses, although severe reactions to routine vaccinations do occur in the breed. Adverse reactions have also been noted when cortisone drugs, flea control products, and some heartworm medications are used. Xolos cannot tolerate the recommended dosages of these drugs. The average life span of a Xolo is twelve to fifteen years.

GENETICS OF HAIRLESSNESS

The Xolo has been judged to be an indigenous American breed, unrelated to hairless dogs of other cultures. This conclusion is based on the study of residual specimens found in South America and Mexico which still possess recognizable breed traits.

Hairlessness is due to a dominant gene; consequently with expression of the recessive gene, coated offspring are expected to occur. Every hairless Xolo can hand down to its progeny either hairlessness or a full coat of hair. Each Hairless carries the (H) dominant hairless gene and the (h) recessive gene for hair. (HH) is a lethal combination, and that is why the hairless gene is called a dominant lethal.

Only (Hh) puppies are born normally as hairless and (hh) puppies as coated, carrying no hairless gene at all This leads to two genetic possibilities for a Xolo, either (Hh) hairless, or (hh) coated. In each case, the dog carries the inherited factor for hair. If a coated dog is mated to a coated bitch, the hairless gene is not present at all.

BREEDING PROGRAMMES

Coated dogs play a critical role in any breeding programme. When a potentially lethal gene is involved, coated dogs are nature's way of insuring the continuation of the breed. The introduction of a coated Xolo into a breeding programme will bring beneficial changes in dentition, substance, and stability of temperament. They play an essential role in maintaining the health and quality of the breed.

In addition to being free of many of the common defects which plague other breeds, Xolos are natural free whelpers, and they are excellent mothers. Xolo puppies are fat, wrinkly, blunt-nosed and short-legged – a far cry from their sleek and statuesque parents. It is amazing to watch the metamorphosis as they develop into lean, muscled and elegant adults. Xolos generally mature by the time they are twelve months old, when they show a calm and dignified outlook on life. Their large expressive ears may take up to a year to become fully erect.

There are just a handful of Xolo breeders in the U.S. today.

Through carefully planned breeding programmes they are working towards refining and maintaining the conformation and health of the breed. An approved breeder referral list is available through the Xoloitzcuintli Club of America.

THE XOLOITZCUINTLI CLUB OF AMERICA

The X.C.A. was formed on October 26, 1986 by a small group of individuals devoted to promoting and protecting this very rare breed As club membership and activity expanded, the decision was made to incorporate the organisation, giving it a more official status in its quest for A.K.C. recognition. Since its inception, the X.C.A. has made a concerted effort to compile background information on American Xolos. The club maintains a computerized registry as part of its record-keeping function, in order to verify the previously undocumented origin of many of these dogs.

Membership in the club is widespread throughout the U.S. The X.C.A. encourages communication between Xolo fanciers worldwide through the bi-monthly publication of the official club newsletter, *The Xolo News*. In this way members are kept up-to-date with news of the club's activities, historical breed information, health and grooming tips and announcements of shows. The club sponsors several shows each year and members are invited to participate in a variety of events in order to gain wider recognition for the breed.

THE AMERICAN HAIRLESS TERRIER

A recent development in America has been the American Hairless Terrier. The first hairless puppy occurred as a mutation in a litter of Rat Terriers.

This hairless gene is recessive, and coated parents will produce hairless offspring. This is totally different to the lethal dominant gene of the Chinese Crested and other Hairless breeds. All terrier puppies are born coated and lose all their hair by six to eight weeks of age. They come in two sizes, toy and miniature, and all have full perfect dentition.

BREED STANDARD OF THE AMERICAN HAIRLESS TERRIER

GENERAL APPEARANCE: The dog's body is neat and trim, resembling a very small deer. The dog's carriage and confident manner should give the appearance of vigor and self-importance. They are very active, lively and alert.

HEIGHT: From withers to ground 10 to 15ins.

WEIGHT: 7 to 14 pounds.

HEAD: Slightly rounded, muzzle medium long, medium stop.

EARS: Erect or tipped. If cropped to a point long and carried erect.

TEETH: Full dentition, level or scissor bite.

EYES: Round, with an alert expression. May be any color.

NOSE: Self-colored.

NECK: Medium length, with a graceful arch.

BODY: Length of body is slightly longer than height, rump curving slightly to tail set. Long and straight front legs, moderately angulated back legs.

TAIL: Carried up or back, may be any length naturally.

FEET: Compact and oval, dewclaws may be removed or left.

SKIN: Warm to the touch, soft smooth. Free from hair except whiskers and eyebrows. Puppies are born with hair. They will begin losing the hair in a week, starting at the nose and receding in a band toward the back until hairless at six to eight weeks. When hot or scared, they will break into a sweat.

COLOR: Partly colored with general color of pink and freckles

*The American
Hairless Terrier*

or spots of contrasting colors. The colors darken with sun; the freckles enlarge with age.

GAIT: Graceful, kind of cocky.

FAULTS: Missing teeth, underbite, overbite, hair on any part of the body other than whiskers or eyebrows.

Reproduced by kind permission of the American Kennel Club.

Chapter Three

THE CHINESE CRESTED

The Chinese Crested has come a long way from its ancient past, and it is hoped that the breed's future is now secure so that many more people will enjoy the company of one of the most extrovert, fascinating and intelligent little toy dogs. The Hairless dog is warm to the touch, and its skin is soft and smooth. It is odourless and will keep itself very clean. If the need arises, a bath takes only a few minutes. The Powderpuff variety does not have a heavy seasonal moult, except when it loses its puppy coat. At this time the dog will need a thorough daily grooming. In Hutchinson's *Dog Encyclopaedia* hairless dogs are described as belonging to the group of greyhounds. Anyone who owns a Chinese Crested will agree that they are extremely "houndy" in character and conformation. They are often suspicious of strangers and many can be quite aloof. A group of them will howl in unison. They have a good turn of speed and will give chase to rabbits and squirrels. In fact, they may well have been used to hunt small game. It is one of the great joys of owning the breed to watch a group of them chasing around a field with crests and plumes flying, looking like small Arab horses.

Chinese Cresteds were imported into Great Britain in the late

Chinese Emperor: Imported into Britain in the late 1800s.

1800s. Mr W. K. Taunton, a collector of rare breeds of dogs, exhibited 'Chinese Emperor' at the Crystal Palace in 1896. He also imported one of the first Afghan Hounds, called Motee. In 1894 *The Kennel Gazette* listed a Hairless Chinese Crested Terrier, called Tangy, in its Foreign Dogs section. It belonged to Mrs T. Barrets. But there was no real attempt to establish the breed in Great Britain. It was regarded as a curiosity, and it was even exhibited in The Zoological Gardens in London.

In 1959 the American Hairless Dog Club was founded by Mrs Debora Wood, owner of the Crest Haven Kennels in Florida. All hairless dogs had been registered by the American Kennel Club, and when this service was discontinued Mrs Wood took on the task herself. She continued this service until her death in 1969, when it was taken over by Paul and Jo Ann Orlik. The influence of Crest Haven Kennels has been far-reaching and dogs from this line are behind nearly all the Chinese Cresteds in Great Britain today.

One of the first to cross the Atlantic was Alta of Crest Haven, a bitch in whelp, imported by the late Mrs Ruth Harris in 1965. Sadly, the puppies did not survive. Further imports also proved fruitless due to abnormalities – apparently roach-backs were a big problem. Four dogs died and the first five litters also failed to survive. The late Mrs Marjorie Mooney, of the well-known Winterlea Kennels in Scotland, imported Wy Ho and Starba from Mrs Wood at this time. She produced some very nice dogs over the years, including Winterlea Regal Choice, Luke Splendid, and Sunbelle, dam of Winterlea Intoo Aes, who proved to be a very dominant sire.

Mrs Harris eventually reared two litters in 1968 which included Staround Atlanta, owned by Mrs Dorothy Tyler, and Staround Cresta, owned by the late Mrs Dorothy Crowther-Davies. In 1969 Mrs Harris imported three dogs from Gypsy Rose Lee, who accompanied them herself. Two dogs and one bitch were added to the Staround kennels, and these included the ten-month-old Staround Ahn Ahn Lee. The combination of the Crest Haven and Lee lines was a great success. Staround Ahn Ahn Lee stamped his make and shape on his progeny, and produced some lovely Cresteds. He was a well-proportioned dog, not a small one, but his type is still favoured.

The Chinese Crested Dog Club was founded in 1969 with Miss

Three early imports from the USA: Winterlea Starba of Crest Haven (above), Nero and his sister Eloa of Crest Haven (right).

Staround Ahn Ahn Lee.

Staround Gala, Cannybuff Cheetah and Staround Brahma, owned by the late Mrs Dorothy Crowther-Davies.

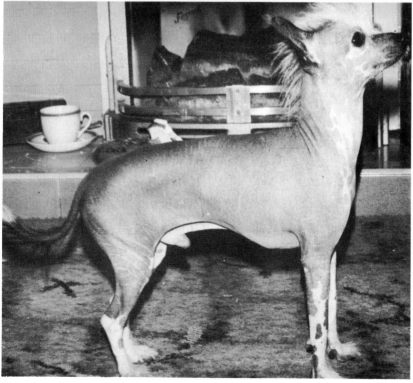

Winterlea Wy Ho of Crest Haven: Imported from the USA by Mrs Marjorie Mooney in 1969.

Staround Cresta: Owned by the late Mrs Dorothy Crowther-Davies.

Staround Inca (Staround Ahn Ahn Lee – Staround Danta), owned by the late Mrs Dorothy Crowther-Davies.

Staround Cresta and Staround Expo.

Lee as president, Mrs Ruth Harris as chairman, Mrs Joan Forster acting as secretary and Mrs Dorothy Tyler as treasurer. The Club's first show was held on September 28th 1974 at Shipley Hall near Wolverhampton, the home of Mrs Dorothy Crowther-Davies. Dorothy, owner of the Cannybuff Kennels, was the judge, and Best In Show went to Mrs Mary Smith's Staround Quanto, who was to win many more top awards during his show career. The Reserve Best in show was Mrs Dorothy Tyler's lovely bitch Staround Tyla, who also went on to be a prolific winner. Both these dogs were of superb type and would have made worthy champions if they had been born a few years later.

At this show a class for Powderpuffs was scheduled, although they were disliked by many breeders. Attempts were made to breed them out by discarding all Powderpuffs from breeding programmes. They were thought of as throwbacks or even mongrels, and they were given away as pets, or even worse, they were destroyed. The stock lost in those early days was irreplaceable. Mrs Iris Phillips campaigned vigorously for the recognition of the Powderpuff as a separate variety and gradually the Powderpuff gained more supporters as people became aware of its importance to the breed. It was extremely frustrating for the exhibitors of Powderpuffs at this time. Although fully registered at the Kennel Club, there was no mention of them in the Interim Standard. Judges had no option other than to examine the dogs and then dismiss them from the ring before making placings.

Eventually in July 1981, at a Special General Meeting, members of the Chinese Crested Dog Club elected to recognise the Powderpuff as a separate variety. A meeting was held at The Kennel Club in November of that year, chaired by Wing Commander Iles, with geneticist Dr Willis and Mr Stockman present. It was attended by the officers and committee of the club: Mr Foster Parker, chairman; Mrs Bowdler-Townsend, secretary; Mrs Olwyn Harbottle, Mr Barrie Jones, Mr and Mrs John Smith, Mr and Mrs Arthur Broadhead and Mrs Irene White. On this historic occasion the breed was recognised as having two separate varieties; it was not to be split into two separate breeds. It was agreed that both types should be shown together.

Unfortunately there are still two camps, pro and anti Powderpuff, but the breed is now settling down and as it gains wider recognition it is able to hold its own in the show ring. A

*Minatura
La Streaker
(Staround
Zorra –
Staround
Yinga)*

Staround Extro and Staround Mr Wonderful, pictured with Bob Brampton.

Staround Java (Staround Ahn Ahn Lee – Staround Brittania).

Acambo's Suzie Wong, photographed at fourteen years old.

second breed club gained Kennel Club approval in January 1988, and the Chinese Crested Club of Great Britain was set up to recognise both varieties, and to try and rid the breed of bias. Its motto is simply 'Together'. At the club's first show Mrs Iris Phillips entered the fifteen-year-old Acambo's Suzie Wong in the veteran class. This was the very Powderpuff she campaigned in the seventies. Sadly, this much-loved Powderpuff died on October 3rd 1989 at the grand old age of sixteen years.

Chapter Four

THE GENETICS OF HAIRLESSNESS

It is important to have some knowledge of the genetics of hairlessness in order to understand the Chinese Crested. There are many excellent books available on this absorbing subject, but my intention is to give the newcomer a basic introduction to this highly specialised area.

There are two varieties of all hairless breeds of dog: those with hair on their bodies – Hairless, and those fully-coated – Powderpuffs. Hairlessness in dogs is the result of an incomplete dominant mutation, which is lethal when homozygous (carrying only the hairless gene). After many generations of hairless-to-hairless breeding the Powderpuff will still appear, as the early breeders discovered. This is because hairlessness in dogs is dominant, and not recessive, as in most mutations. The two varieties are inseparable due to this genetic make-up. Whether you prefer one variety or the other, this fact has to be accepted. In 1930 Letard researched hairlessness, for which we should all be grateful. He found that when two hairless dogs are mated, their homozygous hairless progeny had such extreme abnormalities (absence of ear canals and malformation of the buccal cavity) that few are born alive, and none survive. Every Hairless Chinese Crested carries the dominant gene for hairlessness (Hr – hair on head, feet and tail only), and the gene for normal coat (hr). It is said to be heterozygous. (Hr) is dominant over the recessive (hr), thus a Hairless can be referred to as (Hrhr).

The gene which produces hairlessness is an incomplete dominant lethal. So the unlucky puppy which inherits a double dose of (HrHr) will die in the uterus or soon after birth, due to abnormalities. It is said to be homozygous. The puppy that receives a double dose of (hr), the gene for coat (hrhr) will be a homozygous Powderpuff carrying no hairless gene at all. This is not a lethal combination. It is only a double dose of hairless genes that is lethal. The Chinese Crested can therefore be a Hairless (Hrhr) or a Powderpuff (hrhr). The homozygous puppy, carrying only the Hairless gene (HrHr), does not survive.

Both carry the gene for coat. This is why the Powderpuff cannot be bred out. To calculate a prediction of matings would need data from many litters, and as litter sizes can vary from one to eight puppies, that is probably more than most people would embark on. If you do collect data over the years, the following ratios will be just about right. One factor from each parent is passed to each puppy. The mating of two Hairless Chinese Cresteds (Hrhr) x (Hrhr) would give the predicted result of two Hairless and one Powderpuff: a ratio of 2:1.

(Hr hr) Hairless

	Hr	hr	
Hr	Hr Hr HOMOZYGOUS HAIRLESS **WILL DIE**	Hr hr HETEROZYGOUS HAIRLESS **WILL SURVIVE**	2 Hairless 1 Powderpuff
hr	Hr hr HETEROZYGOUS HAIRLESS **WILL SURVIVE**	hr hr HOMOZYGOUS POWDERPUFF **WILL SURVIVE**	

Hairless

The mating of a Hairless to a Powderpuff (Hrhr) x (hrhr) would give the predicted result of equal Hairless and Powderpuff: a ratio of 1:1.

(Hr hr) Hairless

	Hr hr HETEROZYGOUS HAIRLESS *WILL SURVIVE*	hr hr HOMOZYGOUS POWDERPUFF *WILL SURVIVE*
hr		
Powderpuff		
hr	Hr hr HETEROZYGOUS HAIRLESS *WILL SURVIVE*	hr hr HOMOZYGOUS POWDERPUFF *WILL SURVIVE*

2 Hairless
2 Powderpuffs

The mating of a Powderpuff to a Powderpuff (hrhr) x (hrhr) would result in a litter of Powderpuffs.

(hr hr) Powderpuff

	hr hr HOMOZYGOUS POWDERPUFF *WILL SURVIVE*	hr hr HOMOZYGOUS POWDERPUFF *WILL SURVIVE*
hr		
Powderpuff		
hr	hr hr HOMOZYGOUS POWDERPUFF *WILL SURVIVE*	hr hr HOMOZYGOUS POWDERPUFF *WILL SURVIVE*

4 Powderpuffs

Note these puppies will carry no hairless genes at all.

Nature does not always fit in with these neat calculations in individual litters. Sometimes a Hairless x Hairless, or Hairless x Powderpuff mating will produce all Hairless or all Powderpuff. That is why this breed is so absorbing – it keeps you guessing, and forever intrigued.

VARIABLE EXPRESSIVITY

A further complication to understanding the breed is the amount of hairlessness or hairiness shown in individual dogs. A dominant mutation can show considerable variation of the mutant gene. In the case of the Chinese Crested it is the amount and extent of hairlessness that varies. Genetically hairless dogs can carry varying amounts of hair on their bodies, as well as crest, socks and plume. Therefore, the extent of hairlessness the puppies will inherit is quite unpredictable. The amount of hair on crest, socks and plume can vary from sparse to dense. Others develop hair on their bodies where it is not wanted, and that can be a real headache for breeders.

This variability is unfortunately a characteristic of the incomplete dominant lethal mutation. The extent of this undesired hairiness can vary from a few spare hairs to large patches of hair. There may be a ridge of hair from the base of the neck to the tail. Or hair may grow up the legs beyond the pastern and hock joints, and on to the rump. The hair can sometimes be so abundant that it gives the appearance of pantaloons. At one extreme it may give a fine covering all over the body; the other extreme is that the dog is so hairless that it has virtually no crest, socks or plume. Although these extremes are thought of as a fault in the show ring, after strict selection in the breeding programme, a very hairy Hairless, or a complete 'baldy' may crop up from time to time.

These variants should be thought of as a problem of the dominant mutation requiring discusion, rather than being considered a major fault. The Standard does allow for extreme hairlessness (although not preferred), but not excess hair. The extreme hairy Hairless can look almost like a lightly coated Powderpuff. They have even been referred to as semi-coats, which makes things even more complicated for a newcomer to the breed. In order to check whether such a dog is a genetically Hairless or a Powderpuff, simply look in the mouth. If the dog is genetically Hairless it will have forward-pointing tusks; if it is a Powderpuff it will have a normal mouth. Some people record Hairless puppies being born from Powderpuff x Powderpuff matings, even though such births are not possible; what has happened, most probably, is that a very hairy Hairless has been used. No matter how much hair these dogs have, they will still carry the gene for hairlessness. It is sometimes thought that breeding with Powderpuffs will increase the incidence of unwanted hair on the bodies of the Hairless variety. As Powderpuffs do not carry the hairless gene, they cannot influence the amount of hair or lack of hair in the Hairless dog. It should therefore be accepted that this variation is a natural occurrence and breeders must try to be selective and continue the challenge. There is obviously a lot more to be uncovered on this subject. Perhaps one day someone will do more research into hairlessness in the dog and unlock all the secrets.

An excellent 'Hairless' mouth with forward pointing canine 'tusks'.

Mike Richards.

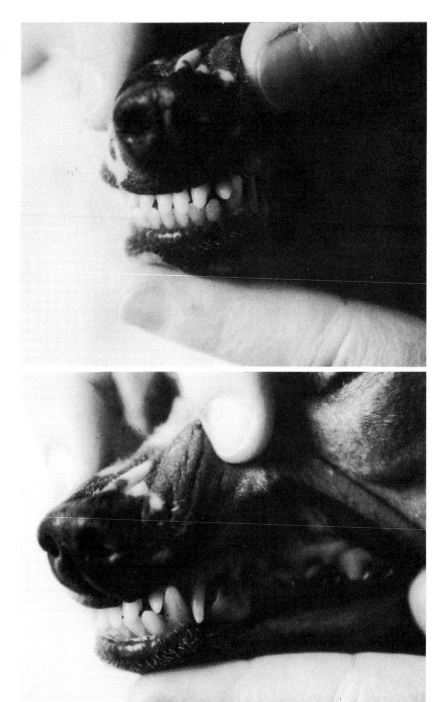

Chapter Five

DENTITION

The dentition of the Chinese Crested is always a subject for lively debate, and all manner of excuses are made for the mouths of Hairless dogs being in a poor state. These range from: "Hairless dogs should have missing teeth", "their mouths are prehistoric", to "by the time the dog is eighteen months old it will have no teeth". When I first started in the breed, I was advised not to worry about mouths. However, I had spent the previous ten years breeding Smooth Fox Terriers, and I was not prepared to accept this. The mouth of the Hairless dog is different from normal canine dentition, but this is really no excuse for accepting mediocrity. Most breeds need some sort of improvement, be it ear carriage, coat, feet or even conformation. The Chinese Crested is no exception; mouths can and have been improved by careful selection. It is the Hairless gene that affects dentition. When Charles Darwin expounded his theory of evolution he stated that in most animals the teeth or horns have some relation to the growth or absence of hair. For example, both pigs and elephants have forward-pointing tusks.

The Powderpuff carries no Hairless genes, and therefore it has a normal canine mouth. At the front there are six incisors top and bottom. The canine teeth are strong and slightly curved. Behind the canine teeth are four pre-molars and two molars, in both upper and lower jaws. This makes forty-two teeth in all, in a tight scissor bite. The Hairless mouth is different from that of the Powderpuff, but unfortunately the new Breed Standard does not refer to this very important fact at all. The teeth of the Hairless variety differ in shape from those in a normal mouth. The canines are conical and point forward; they are referred to as tusks. This is a characteristic which applies to both good and bad "Hairless" mouths.

The shape of the incisors can vary considerably. Some are no more than little pegs protruding from the gums. Others are almost normal. Sometimes a full complement of narrow 'pegs' can look as if they have been thrown in haphazardly. The number of teeth present can also vary. In the worst example, many can be missing, having never been present at all.

Occasionally, milk teeth which showed great promise are not replaced with adult teeth; and where milk teeth have been

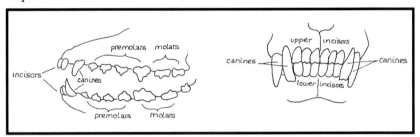

missing, adult teeth can appear! The teeth that are present can be poorly rooted. For example, incisors may point forward like the tusks, but they will certainly fall out at an early age. Pre-molars will be missing in the Hairless variety – one, two, or maybe all of them. Even a good Hairless mouth may be without first and second pre-molars, and this should be accepted as normal. Tusks and missing pre-molars are not mentioned in the Standard, but these characteristics should be acknowledged as typical of the Hairless mouth.

There are those who advocate that the Chinese Crested mouth should not be examined by judges. In my opinion, this is quite ridiculous, as the problem can be solved by careful, selective breeding. This has been achieved, and therefore it is a goal that all breeders should work towards. There is plenty of room in the

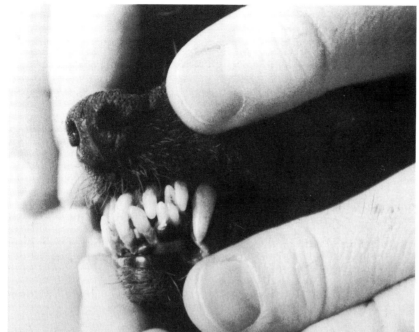

A very poor 'Hairless' mouth with missing and crammed incisors.

Mike Richards.

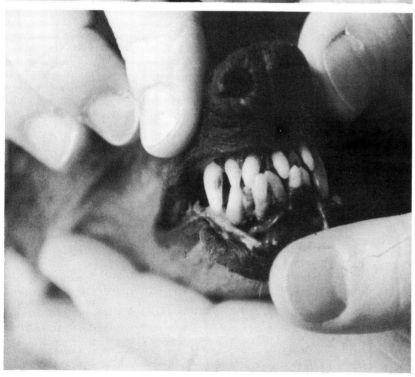

Chinese Crested mouth for its teeth, for the dog has a normal-shaped head and a good length of foreface.

It will take time and patience to get the right result, but it is well worth the effort. The old Interim Standard and the New American Standard also fail to include these important facts concerning dentition. In fact, the original American Standard stated that missing teeth should not be a deciding factor in judging the breed. This has been amended in the latest edition, indicating that improvement is sought. It is sometimes thought that the inclusion of a Powderpuff in the breeding programme will improve dentition, because they have normal mouths. They do not carry the Hairless gene so their mouths are not affected by the mutation. But before using a Powderpuff in a breeding programme you must check its Hairless brothers and sisters, if at all possible. Not all Powderpuffs are perfect specimens; some do not have the correct scissor bite. The Powderpuff must not be thought of as a magician who can cure all faults – the laws of all dog breeding apply here. Look out for undershot and overshot mouths, as well as missing teeth.

A successful breeding programme to improve dentition will result in a mouth where all the incisors are evenly placed in each jaw. One or two pre-molars may be missing. The forward-pointing tusks will still remain, but the teeth will be of better quality, and they will not fall out in eighteen months time. Despite all this effort, it must be said that a good mouth will not last as long as in other breeds. By the time the dog is five years old the teeth will be loosening, but this is still a vast improvement.

Chapter Six

THE BRITISH
BREED STANDARD

BREED STANDARD FOR THE CHINESE CRESTED

GENERAL APPEARANCE: A small, active and graceful dog; medium to fine boned, smooth hairless body, with hair on feet, head and tail only. Or covered with a soft veil of hair.

CHARACTERISTICS: Two distinct types of this breed: deer type, racy and fine boned, and cobby type, heavier in body and bone.

TEMPERAMENT: Happy, never vicious.

HEAD AND SKULL: Slightly rounded and elongated skull. Cheeks cleanly chiselled, lean and flat, tapering into muzzle. Stop slightly pronounced but not too extreme. Head smooth, without excess wrinkles. Distance from base of skull to stop equal to distance from stop to tip of nose. Muzzle tapering slightly but never pointed, lean without flews. Nose a prominent feature, narrow in keeping with muzzle. Any colour nose acceptable.

Head presenting graceful appearance, with alert expression. Lips tight and thin. Ideally, crest beginning at stop, tapering off down neck. Crest itself may flow to any length, a long and flowing crest preferred, but sparse acceptable.

EYES: So dark as to appear black; little or no white showing; medium size; set wide apart.

EARS: Set low: highest point of base of ear level with outside corner of eye. Large and erect, with or without fringe, except in the Powderpuffs where drop ears are permissible.

MOUTH: Jaws strong, with perfect, regular scissor bite, i.e. the upper teeth closely overlapping the lower teeth and set square into jaws.

NECK: Lean, free from throatiness, long and sloping gracefully into strong shoulders. When moving, carried high and slightly arched.

FOREQUARTERS: Shoulders clean, narrow and well laid back. Legs long and slender, set well under the body. Elbows held close to body. Pasterns fine, strong, nearly vertical. Toes turned neither in nor out.

BODY: Medium to long. Supple. Chest rather broad and deep, not barrel-ribbed. Breast bone not prominent. Brisket extending to elbows; moderate tuck-up.

HINDQUARTERS: Rump well rounded and muscular, loins taut, stifles fine and long, sweeping smoothly into the well let-down hock. Angulation of the rear limb must be such as to produce a level back. Hind-legs set wide apart.

FEET: Extreme hare foot, narrow and very long, with unique elongation of the small bones between joints, especially in the forefeet, which almost appear to possess an extra joint. Nails any colour, moderately long. Socks ideally confined to toes, but not extending above top of pastern. Feet turning neither in nor out.

TAIL: Set high, carried up or out when in motion. Long and tapering, fairly straight, not curled or twisted to either side, falling naturally when at rest. Plume long and flowing, confined to the lower two-thirds of the tail. Sparse plume acceptable.

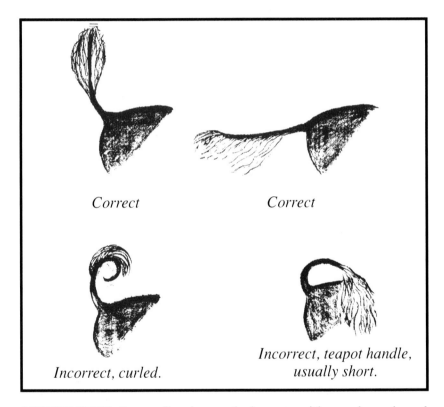

Correct   *Correct*

Incorrect, curled.

Incorrect, teapot handle, usually short.

MOVEMENT: Long, flowing and elegant, with good reach and plenty of drive.

COAT: No large patches of hair anywhere on body. Skin fine-grained, smooth, warm to touch. In Powderpuffs coat consists of an undercoat with soft veil of long hair; veil coat a feature.

COLOUR: Any colour or combination of colours.

SIZE: Ideal height in dogs: 28-33 cms (11-13 ins) at withers. Bitches: 23-30 cms (9-12 ins) at withers. Weight varies considerably, but should not be over 5 kgs (12 lbs).

FAULTS: Any departure from the foregoing points should be considered a fault and the seriousness of the fault should be in exact proportion to its degree.

NOTE: Male animals should have two apparently normal testicles fully descended into the scrotum.

Reproduced by kind permission of The English Kennel Club.

The Breed Standard is sparse in its description, and in some instances, I believe there are serious omissions. I have therefore enlarged upon these aspects, for after all, the Breed Standard lies at the foundation of every breed, and it is vital that a fair and accurate picture is presented.

CHARACTERISTICS

The British Breed Standard states that there are two types of Chinese Crested: the deer type, which is racy and fine-boned, and the cobby, which is heavier in body and bone, but it does not give separate descriptions. In fact, they are very different in appearance. The cobby is 'rounder' in most departments – eyes, skull, bone, rib-cage – and they are shorter on the leg. It is certainly not an elegant dog, and therefore it is a contradiction of the Standard. In fact, there are very few true deer or cobby types seen in the show ring these days. The type now exhibited is a combination of the two.

TEMPERAMENT

The Chinese Crested should never be vicious or aggressive, according to the Standard. However, they can be apprehensive of strangers, and rather aloof in their manner, which is a

Cobby type.

Deer type.

Skeleton of the Chinese Crested showing balanced head, clean throat, erect ears, arched neck, well-laid shoulder, level topline, well let down hocks, extreme hare foot.

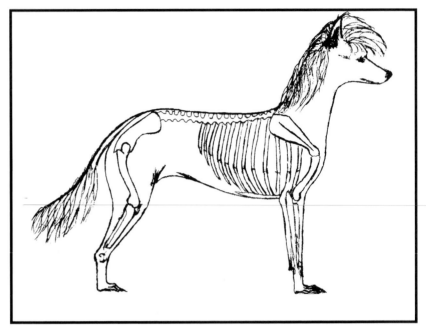

characteristic of some hounds. This should not be confused with timidity or aggression. The most calm and stable dog can pull back from a judge bending down to it, and this characteristic is not uncommon in toy dogs.

HEAD AND SKULL

A sparse crest is clearly stated as being acceptable. Many judges overlook a well-made dog with sparse crest for another with plenty of furnishings, but lacking elegance and soundness. Those with sparse crests usually have the most lovely soft, smooth skin. They should not be penalised on this point alone.

EYES

The Standard gives no indication as to the shape of the eye. It tends to be round in the cobby and almond-shaped in the deer type. The American Standard, which forms the basis of the British Standard, calls for almond-shaped eyes, which are typical in the majority of the breed. A round eye on a deer type would give a very "foreign" expression.

EARS

The Standard clearly states that the ears may be dropped in the Powderpuff, and indeed, the majority of Powderpuff ears are dropped. There are those that would like to stipulate that ears should be erect in both varieties, but it is rare for a Powderpuff to have erect ears. A drop-eared Powderpuff will have Hairless litter mates with strong erect ears, and trimming off ear fringes to remove weight of hair will not increase the number of true erect ears in a litter.

MOUTH

The main omission here is the difference between the Hairless and Powderpuff mouth. No mention is made of the shape of teeth, the forward-pointing tusks, or the missing pre-molars in the Hairless. The Standard's basic requirements of strong jaws with perfect regular scissor bite can be met, but the unique differences should be accepted and mentioned. Judges often put a Hairless down because they are uncertain about what they should be looking for.

FOREQUARTERS

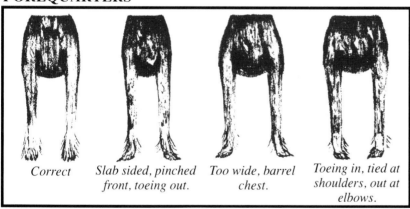

Correct   *Slab sided, pinched front, toeing out.*   *Too wide, barrel chest.*   *Toeing in, tied at shoulders, out at elbows.*

A well-laid shoulder is required, but there is no mention of the length and angle of the upper arm. To achieve the desired long, flowing movement, the upper arm needs to be almost as long as the shoulder blade. The two should make an angle of 90 degrees. Toes should not turn in or out, according to the Standard, but this is often overlooked when the breed is being judged.

45° *Correct shoulder placement will give a long arched neck and free-flowing extended front action.*

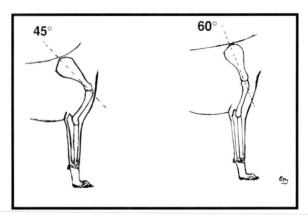

60° *Incorrect straight shoulder and upper arm. neck will be short, front movement will lack reach if upper arm is short, and will be Hackneyed.*

BODY

The Standard calls for a medium to long body, but this does not mean we are looking for a dog which is short on the leg. Legs should be long and slender, giving the balance of a running hound. Neither a short-backed terrier type nor a dachshund type is desirable.

HINDQUARTERS

The requirement for hindquarters to be set wide apart is a source of constant uncertainty. The new American Standard has been

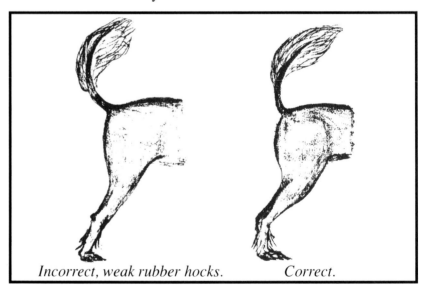

Incorrect, weak rubber hocks.   *Correct.*

amended to state that hocks should be set well apart, which makes better sense. Many of the world's top winning and well-constructed Cresteds could never meet this requirement, as far as the hindquarters are concerned, yet they still have vertical hocks when standing. Unfortunately, both Standards make no reference to the problem of rubber hocks. These are unsightly, and usually go with weak tucked-up hindquarters.

FEET

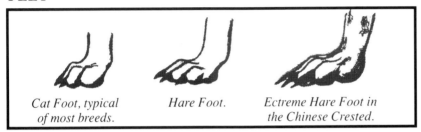

Cat Foot, typical of most breeds.

Hare Foot.

Ectreme Hare Foot in the Chinese Crested.

The description of the Chinese Crested foot is very good, except for "socks confined to toes". If a full crest is preferred, there will certainly be more hair on the feet. Hair is confined to the toes only in the sparsely furnished Crested.

MOVEMENT

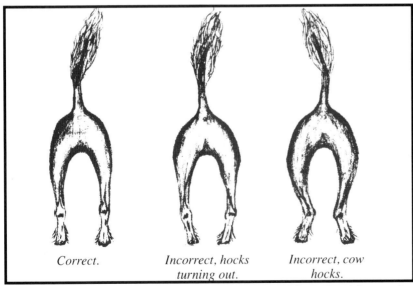

Correct.

Incorrect, hocks turning out.

Incorrect, cow hocks.

The long flowing movement cannot be achieved without the

correct front and hind angulation. Weak tucked-up hindquarters have no drive, and incorrect hackney action is often seen from short, steep upper arms and upright shoulders. This will fail to give the necessary extension to achieve flowing movement.

COAT

Due to the variable expressivity of the hairless gene, it is almost impossible to eliminate sparse hair in the Crested. Selective breeding can help, but it is a feature we have to live with. The coat of the Powderpuff causes confusion. The Standard calls for an undercoat with a soft veil of long hair. It is only in recent years that the Powderpuff coat has been given real coat care, so we are only just seeing the beauty of the mature coat. The length of coat will vary: if the Hairless in the line have long crests, the coat will be long; if they are sparsely crested, the coat will be thinner and shorter. The coat is made up of long, soft hairs with coarser guard hairs. When the dog is young these hairs are short and look like an undercoat, but by the time the dog is eighteen months old, they grow through to create the so-called veil. In reality, this is not a very good description and it causes much confusion among judges and breeders. On a well-groomed dog the guard hairs will mingle with the main coat and they will only show if they are a darker colour, which gives a very attractive appearance.

An extremely hairy Hairless will fit the Standard, which has also led to confusion. There is another coat-type, which is seen occasionally. It is shorter and quite coarse. The ears are also smaller than normal and are erect. These types are probably the result of mixed parentage, way back in the evolution of the breed.

COLOUR

The Chinese Crested comes in an attractive variety of shades, ranging from blue to mahogany (liver). The darkest 'blue' can be almost black, paling to lighter shades of steel-blue, elephant-grey, and lilac (pale blue/grey). The mahogany shades can be richly coloured, paling through to honey. These solid colours are often broken up on the chest, legs and under-belly with pink

Amber of Stevansu : A heavily-coated Powderpuff.

Pearce.

Zebedi; An erect eared short-coated Powderpuff.

Staround Navaro of Zucci: A young blue dog of excellent type.

Gorman's Kiwi Razzmatazz: Typifying a spotted Chinese Crested.

unpigmented skin. This gives a mottled effect known as lacing, which is very attractive. The colours of the spotted types can be any of the above shades, with a pink background.

The depth and richness of colour varies with the seasons. Chinese Cresteds love to sunbathe and their skin will reach full colour in the summer. During the winter, or when the skin is not exposed to sunlight, the pigment will fade. It is surprising how quickly the colour will develop again after the winter.

The Powderpuff coat is predominantly pale gold, paling through to cream and white. Black and whites are occasionally seen, the white generally being on the chest, socks and the tip of the tail. Some puppies are born with black and white coats, but these usually grow through to be cream or white at maturity, with a little colour remaining on the ear fringes. A sabling effect is produced by darker guard hairs growing through once the coat has reached maturity.

The overall appearance and expression of the Chinese Crested is enhanced if the dog has good pigmentation on the nose and around the eyes, although this is not a requirement in the Standard.

SIZE

Size and weight vary considerably. This could be the result of better rearing, although the early imports were a mix of large and small dogs. A deer and cobby of the same height will have very different weights. A cobby standing at thirteen inches would come within the height stipulated in the Standard, but it will certainly be overweight. An experienced judge will assess the whole dog, and will penalise if there is any coarseness in the make-up.

Am. Ch. Razzmatazz Strelka.

Gipez's Joie de Vivre. Note the trimmed ears.

Barber Studios

Chapter Seven

THE CHINESE CRESTED IN AMERICA

It was not until the late 19th century that the Chinese Crested started to feature in the show world, and there are accounts of both varieties of the breed in the literature of the day. The Hairless and the Powderpuff were exhibited at one of the earliest dog shows in America – the fourth annual Westminster Show. According to a show catalogue from 1885, two Cresteds were exhibited in the Miscellaneous class at the ninth annual New York Benched Show. During those early years Cresteds were bred and exhibited sporadically by just a handful of fanciers.

THE AMERICAN HAIRLESS DOG CLUB

Shortly after the First World War, Mrs Wood of Homestead, Florida started her famous Crest Haven Kennel. Nearly every line of Chinese Cresteds in existence today traces its beginnings back to this line. At that time no formal registry existed for the breed, and Mrs Wood began keeping stud books for her own

*Am. Ch. China
Crest Mohawk
with his sons Am.
Ch. Lejo's
Vladimir and Am.
Ch. Wenlo's
Kuquai Kumquat.*

Bruce Harkins.

*Am. Ch. Kojak
King of the
Blues: Sire of
ten American
Champions.*

breeding programme. By 1946 this effort had grown to include the breeding records of several other Crested kennels, and in 1956 when the Mexican Hairless lost its A.K.C. status it was also included in Mrs Wood's registry. Eventually this expanded into The American Hairless Dog Club. It is quite likely that without Mrs Wood's dedication to promoting and perpetuating the breed, the Chinese Crested would now be extinct. Throughout the Fifties and Sixties Cresteds were seldom exhibited in the Miscellaneous class, and no national club existed to promote the breed. Interest in the breed waned, and in 1965 the A.K.C. announced that the American Hairless Dog Club, which then operated a registry for all hairless breeds, did not conform to its requirements for recognised breeds. Mrs Wood was adamantly opposed to a club and registry exclusively for Chinese Cresteds, and she refused to relinquish her registration books. At this point, the Chinese Crested lost its eligibility for the Miscellaneous class.

THE QUEST FOR AMERICAN KENNEL CLUB RECOGNITION

After Mrs Wood's death in 1969, the studbooks and remaining Crest Haven dogs were purchased from her heirs. In 1979 the American Chinese Crested Club was founded. This registry, which began with Mrs Wood's records, now includes almost two thousand dogs.

The Club has worked towards satisfying the A.K.C. requirements for recognition. In September 1985 the A.K.C. voted to readmit the Chinese Crested, and in February 1986 the breed became eligible for the Miscellaneous class. The breed gains full A.K.C. acceptance in 1991, which is a great achievement. The original American Standard was excellent, paying great attention to detail. Unfortunately, it has now been replaced with a much shorter version.

THE NEW AMERICAN BREED STANDARD FOR THE CHINESE CRESTED

In the Summer of 1990 a new Breed Standard was submitted to all members of The American Chinese Crested Club. Members had to approve the New Standard prior to The American Kennel

Am. Ch.
Razzmatazz Spike
(left) and Am. Ch.
Razzmatazz
Fleidermaus.

Bruce Harkins.

Razzmatazz
Pekoe of Jann
(Am. Ch. China
Crest Mohawk –
Am Ch. Gipez
Joie de Vive):
to date the only
Powderpuff to
win Best of
Winners at a
Variety Show.

Club officially recognising the breed. As with the previous Standard, it gives a far more detailed description of the Chinese Crested than the British version. Unfortunately, the previous excellent description of the Hairless mouth is now omitted. The absence of teeth is still permitted in the Hairless variety, although there has been a great improvement in recent years. Powderpuff ears are still required to be erect, despite having to be assisted in most cases. Note that a stilted or hackneyed gait is to be faulted, which is an unfortunate omission in the English Standard. The combination of the two Standards give an excellent, full description of the Chinese Crested.

NEW AMERICAN BREED STANDARD

I. GENERAL APPEARANCE: A toy dog, fine-boned, elegant and graceful. The distinct varieties are born in the same litter. The Hairless with hair only on the head, tail and feet and the Powderpuff, completely covered with hair. The breed serves as a loving companion, playful and entertaining.

II. SIZE, PROPORTION AND SUBSTANCE
SIZE: Ideally 11 to 13 inches. However, dogs that are slightly larger or smaller may be given full consideration.
PROPORTION: Proportion rectangular – proportioned to allow for freedom of movement. Body length from withers to base of tail is slightly longer than the height at the withers.
SUBSTANCE: Fine-boned and slender but not so refined as to appear breakable, or alternatively, not a robust, heavy structure.

III. HEAD
EXPRESSION: Alert and intense.
EYES: Almond-shaped, set wide apart. Dark-colored dogs have dark-colored eyes and lighter-colored dogs may have lighter-colored eyes. Eye rims match the coloring of the dog.
EARS: Uncropped large and erect, placed so that the base of the ear is level with the outside corner of the eye.
SKULL: The skull is arched gently over the occiput from ear to ear. Distance from occiput to stop equal to distance from stop to tip of nose. The head is wedge-shaped viewed from above and the side.

STOP: Slight but distinct.

MUZZLE: Cheeks taper cleanly into the muzzle.

NOSE: Dark in dark-colored dogs; may be lighter in lighter-colored dogs. Pigment is solid.

LIPS: Lips are clean and tight.

BITE: Scissor or level in both varieties. Missing teeth in the Powderpuff is to be faulted. The Hairless variety is not to be penalized for absence of full dentition.

IV. NECK, TOPLINE AND BODY

NECK: Neck is lean and clean, slightly arched from the withers to the base of the skull and carried high.

TOPLINE: Level to slightly sloping croup.

BODY: Brisket extends to the elbow. Breastbone is not prominent. Ribs are well developed. The depth of the chest tapers to a moderate tuck-up at the flanks. Light in loin.

TAIL: Tail is slender and tapers to a curve. It is long enough to reach the hock. When dog is in motion, the tail is carried gaily and may be carried slightly forward over the back. At rest, the tail is down with a slight curve upward at the end resembling a sickle. In the Hairless variety, two-thirds of the end of the tail is covered by long, flowing feathering, referred to as a plume. The Powderpuff variety's tail is completely covered with hair.

V. FOREQUARTERS

ANGULATION: Layback of shoulders is 45 degrees to point of shoulder allowing for good reach.

SHOULDERS: Clean and narrow.

ELBOWS: Close to body.

LEGS: Long, slender and straight.

PASTERNS: Upright, fine and strong. Dewclaws may be removed.

FEET: Hare foot, narrow with elongated toes. Nails are trimmed to moderate length.

VI. HINDQUARTERS

ANGULATION: Stifle moderately angulated. From hock joint to ground perpendicular. Dewclaws may be removed.

FEET: Same as forequarters.

VII. COAT

The Hairless variety has hair on certain portions of the body: the head (called a crest), the tail (called a plume) and the feet from the toes to the front pasterns and rear hock joints (called socks). The texture of all hair is soft and silky, flowing to any length. Placement of hair is not as important as overall type. Areas that have hair usually taper off slightly. Wherever the body is hairless, the skin is soft and smooth.

HEAD CREST: Begins at the stop and tapers off between the base of the skull and the back of the neck. Hair on the ears and face is permitted on the hairless and may be trimmed for neatness in both varieties.

TAIL PLUME: Described under Tail.

The Powderpuff variety is completely covered with a double soft and silky coat. Close examination reveals long, thin guard hairs over the short silky undercoat. The coat is straight, of moderate density and length. Excessively heavy, kinky or curly coat is to be penalized. Grooming is minimal – consisting of presenting a clean and neat appearance.

VII. COLOR: Any color or combination of colors.

IX. GAIT: Lively, agile and smooth without being stilted or hackneyed. Comes and goes at a trot moving in a straight line.

X. TEMPERAMENT: Gay and alert.

The new American Breed Standard forms a good basis for the breed. There are, however, some areas which the new Standard does not cover in so much detaill, and it is worth going back to the original Standard.

THE ORIGINAL AMERICAN BREED STANDARD

HAIRLESS

GENERAL APPEARANCE: A slender fine-boned, active and graceful little dog, with a smooth, hairless body, and hair on head, feet and tail.

TEMPERAMENT: Gay and intelligent, yet at the same time dignified and unaggressive. Faults: Viciousness.

SIZE: Ideal height in males 11 to 13 inches at the withers; females 9 to 12 inches at the withers. Being a toy breed, a smaller dog of equal or superior type should be given full consideration. Faults: The Crested presents a sleek elegant appearance, therefore overweight and /or coarse dogs should be penalised.
DISQUALIFICATIONS: Dogs or bitches over 14 inches at the withers.

WEIGHT: Should not exceed 10 pounds in proportion to the height of the dog.
DISQUALIFICATIONS: Over 12 pounds.

HEAD: Slightly rounded and elongated skull with ears set low. Top of base of the ear is level with the outside corner of the eye. Cheeks are cleanly chiseled, lean and flat, and taper into the muzzle. Stop is pronounced, but not extreme. The head is smooth without excess wrinkles. Distance from the base of skull to stop is equal to the distance from stop to tip of nose. The muzzle tapers slightly without coming to a tip, and is clean, without flews. The nose is a prominent feature, narrow in keeping with the muzzle. Any color nose is acceptable. Overall the head should present a graceful appearance, with alert expression, and no suggestion of coarseness or raciness. Lips are tight and thin. Faults: dished face; too wrinkled skin; snipey muzzle.

EARS: Large and erect, ear leather thin, with ear fringe permitted. Faults: Round or bat ear.
DISQUALIFICATIONS: Broken down or cropped ears.

EYES: So dark as to appear black. Little or no white to show. No sign of dullness. Prominent but not bulging. Almond-shaped, and set wide apart. Faults: Wall eye; Light eye; Eyes set too close.

TEETH: Level or scissor bite. The canine teeth extend slightly forward. Premolars absent. The primitive dentition, linked with

the hairless factor in this variety, causes weak and/or teeth with thin enamel. Therefore, although strong teeth should be encouraged, the condition of the teeth, or missing teeth, should not be a deciding factor in judging this breed.
DISQUALIFICATIONS: Very much undershot.

NECK: Lean and free from throatiness. Long and graceful. When moving, the neck is carried high and slightly arched to the head, sloping gradually into strong withers.
Faults: Ewe neck.

BODY: Supple, smooth and hairless, the skin is fine grained, smooth and warm to touch. The shoulders are clean and narrow, with the blades sloping back to form an angle with the forearm of about 90 degrees. The chest is rather broad and deep, but the ribcage should not be sprung. The breastbone is not overly prominent. Brisket should extend to the elbows, tapering into a moderate tuck-up. The width of the flank does not extend past the elbows when viewed from above. Top line is level. Length of body should be slightly greater than the height at the withers.
Fault: Too refined, lacking in bone development, roach back, sway back, hips considerably higher or lower than withers, square or long bodied dogs.

TAIL: Set high on back and carried either up or out when in motion. Long and tapering, fairly straight, not curled or twisted to either side. Tail should be allowed to fall naturally, when at rest or standing for examination.
Faults: Ring or corkscrew tail, carried low or between the legs when in motion.

FORELEGS: Long and slender, set nicely under the body, long enough to present an elegant stride. The elbows are well knit, held close to the body, and work cleanly and evenly. Pasterns are fine but strong, nearly vertical.Toes turning neither in nor out. Movement is long and flowing, with good reach.
Faults: Pinched front, out at the elbows, hackneyed movement.

HINDLEGS: The slim stifle is moderately angulated; well rounded, muscular rump. Loins taut. Stifles are firm and long,

blending into well let down hocks. The hock extends in a line parallel to the base of tail, but beyond. There is sufficient angulation to produce a level back. Hind legs are set wide apart. The rear presents a driving movement.
Faults: Rubber hocks, slipped stifle, cow hock.

FEET: Extreme hare foot, narrow and very long, with a unique elongation of the small bones between the joints in the toes, especially in the forefeet, which almost appear to possess an extra joint, which in fact they do not. Nails are moderately long. Nails may be colour of toes, or black or white.
Faults: Any other than hare foot.

COLOR: Any color or combination of colors.

CREST: Ideally, the crest begins at the stop, and the hair roots stop growing at the base of the skull. Although permitted to be more extensve, the hair roots should definitely have tapered off by a point no further than one-third of the way down the neck. The hair itself may flow to any length, with a long flowing crest preferred. Texture is soft and silky, being slightly softer in the smaller dogs and slightly coarser in the larger dogs.

SOCKS: Ideally confined to the toes, but should definitely not come above the pastern joint.

PLUME: Long and flowing, but confined to the lower two-thirds of the tail.

HAIR PLACEMENT: Exact hair placement is not as important as overall type. The areas with the hair usually taper off slightly, and the dog with a few stray hairs when shown, in the natural state, is far preferable to one that has been trimmed.
Faults: Large patches of thick hair anywhere on the body, evidence of shaving.

POWDERPUFF

The Standard for the Powderpuff is identical to that of the Hairless except for the following:

GENERAL APPEARANCE: A slender, fine-boned, active graceful little dog, with a soft veil of hair all over, so that it lives up to its Powderpuff name.

EARS: Large, thin ear leather. Ears may be erect or drop, due to weight of hair; if they do drop, both should be down to the same degree. Ear fringes may be trimmed, if desired, to allow ears to stand.
DISQUALIFICATIONS: Cropped ears.

TEETH: Level or scissor bite. Teeth are strong and straight.
Faults: Crooked teeth.
DISQUALIFICATIONS: Very much undershot or overshot.

COAT: Undercoat is very short; guard coat is thin and much longer, giving a definite veil-like effect. A longish coat is preferred, but should never be so long as to hamper movement. Texture is soft and silky, being slightly softer in the smaller dogs, and slightly coarser in the larger dogs. The Powderpuff is shown naturally, without part or bows.

Reproduced by kind permission of the American Kennel Club.

Chinese Crested puppies.

Chapter Eight

BREEDING

Serious thought should always be given before embarking on breeding a litter. Anyone considering breeding Chinese Cresteds should accept both varieties. To attempt to breed just one variety will certainly damage the breed. Breeding dogs for the right reasons is a fascinating hobby, consuming both your time and money – and time, in particular, is something you have to be prepared to give. Breeders are the guardians of their chosen breed for a few short years. It is our responsibility to hand the breed on to future generations improved, but not altered. The aim is not to pander to the fads and fancies of show judges.

The first, and most important step is to buy the best bitch you can afford, and then be prepared to wait patiently. There is no such thing as a perfect specimen, but imperfections should not be too serious nor too numerous. Breeding is about producing sound puppies that conform to the Standard, and the quality of the stock should improve with each generation. If you made a mistake with your first purchase, have the courage to start again, for the sake of the breed.

When it comes to choosing a stud dog, always use a sire who excels where your bitch fails. For example, if she is too big, don't select a small dog. Find a good dog of ideal size. It is well worth the effort to spend time around the shows watching the dogs in competition before making your choice. Don't forget the importance of temperament – this should be high on your list of priorities. It is a good idea to seek advice from the person who bred your bitch; they will know her bloodlines, and may well have a dog that is suitable. The ideal way of improving stock is to keep within a proven bloodline. Remember, a pedigree is just a piece of paper with names on it. It becomes valuable when it is used as a basis for research so that you can discover the faults and qualities of the dogs in that particular line. This takes time and patience, but you will be rewarded in the end. If you decide to out-breed to an unrelated dog, you will have to research even more thoroughly. The best way of doing this is to see as many of the dog's progeny from different bitches as you can. Don't use the first dog that takes your fancy, or the one that lives conveniently near to your home.

I am a keen advocate of line breeding, and of careful in-breeding with good stock. If you use good dogs, success is within your grasp. It is very satisfying to breed a team of sound animals, true to type, which are the result of a carefully planned breeding programme. A high flyer from a chance mating will seldom breed on. You must also be realistic about the time it takes to achieve these results. A top-class stud dog cannot achieve miracles and cure all your bitch's faults in the first litter. Indeed, he may well introduce some faults, if you have not done your research properly.

Now for the options which cause so much controversy in this unique breed. Do you mate a Hairless male to a Hairless female, a Powderpuff male to a Hairless female, a Hairless male to a Powderpuff female, or a Powderpuff male to a Powderpuff female? Some breeders will only ever do Hairless x Hairless matings, as they are totally against the use of Powderpuffs. That is their choice. Others prefer to use a Powderpuff occasionally, which is our preference. There are others who use a Powderpuff male or female at every mating. The careful and sensible use of the Powderpuff will reduce the number of homozygous Hairless, which are lost.

A Powderpuff x Powderpuff mating makes an obvious statement that only Powderpuffs are planned in the litter, thus treating the Powderpuff as a separate breed. However, the Powderpuff is not a separate breed, and the question arises as to whether it is ethical to attempt to breed the Powderpuff exclusively. After the long campaign to have the Powderpuff recognised for the benefit of the breed, the danger of exploitation cannot be ruled out. Powderpuffs are extremely attractive little dogs and could easily find themselves being bred for the pet market, as other breeds have been in the past. This has happened in a small way already. Hairless x Hairless and Hairless x Powderpuff matings keep the ratio of Hairless to Powderpuff at around 2:1 and 1:1 respectively. An increase in Powderpuff x Powderpuff matings could cause a dangerous imbalance in the breed, whose numbers are low compared with other breeds.

The Powderpuff has survived, despite being discarded in the past, because normal matings always produce Powderpuffs. The Hairless could be in danger if the Powderpuff to Powderpuff matings got out of hand. Hopefully, this will not happen, but the possibility needs discussing and breeders should be aware of the dangers.

When you have chosen the stud dog you want to use, book the dog well in advance with the owner. There is nothing more annoying than having someone telephone out of the blue, with a bitch ready for mating, and there has been no prior warning. It is also important to draw up a short written contract, with a signed copy for both you and the stud-keeper. The question may arise as to whether your bitch should receive a free service if she fails to produce pups after the first mating. In actuality, you are paying for the service, and not the guarantee of puppies, but most breeders will offer a repeat mating in this situation. In some instances, the stud fee is exchanged for a puppy. It should be made clear whether this is to be pick of the litter, a dog or a bitch, a Hairless or a Powderpuff. This may seem like a lot of red tape, but many a good friendship has been lost over a simple misunderstanding.

The frequency of seasons varies considerably between individuals. Some bitches come into season every six months, others may go as long as nine months. Hairless bitches often develop spots on their legs and backs at the approach of a season. This will give you about three weeks warning. If you plan a litter it is essential that you know the exact date that your bitch begins her season. If you are using a stud dog from outside your kennel, contact the owner to give plenty of notice of your impending visit. The owner may like your bitch to come early so as not to miss her most suitable day for mating. On the whole, the twelfth to the fourteenth day is the ideal time for mating. There are always exceptions, and some bitches are ready as early as six days or as late as twenty days. The perfect day for mating is when the bitch stops showing colour, this is usually accompanied by much flirting – even with fellow bitches! Make sure you keep your bitch away from all other male dogs at this time – one of our bitches always made a play for our Japanese Akita!

Chinese Cresteds have very few problems during mating. A Powderpuff bitch will benefit from having some coat removed from around the tail, if she is heavily coated. Maidens will soon get the idea after a few 'misses', as long as you remain patient, and speak to them kindly at all times. Our stud dogs tend to take command of the situation immediately. Once mating has taken place and the pair is tied, most dogs will turn themselves so that both tails are together. This is the time when you should make yourself comfortable so you can hold the two together, and prevent them from pulling apart. A tie can last as long as forty minutes, or it may be all over in five minutes. When you are satisfied that mating has been completed, sponge the dog with a mild liquid antiseptic, and put the bitch to rest in her travelling box, if possible. I like to repeat the mating after twenty-four hours, just to make sure, but this is not essential. If you are using a stud dog from outside your kennel, the owner will need to sign the Kennel Club form confirming the date of the mating, and the registration number of the stud. This is also the time to pay any fee that has been agreed.

Chapter Nine

WHELPING AND WEANING

After a successful mating, keep your bitch to her normal diet for at least four to five weeks. There is no need to change or increase her food or alter her daily routine at all. If you allow her to become overweight, this will lead to problems at whelping time. The ideal procedure is to gradually increase the bitch's food when she is around five weeks in-whelp. By this time her 'tuck-up' will be less defined, and there will be signs of a widening behind the ribs. At around seven weeks the puppies can be seen moving and kicking. The bitch's mammary glands will be swelling, and in the Hairless a well-defined 'milk line' can be seen along the flank and veins supplying this area.

When the bitch is getting close to her whelping date, she will prefer a higher percentage of meat in her diet. If she loses her appetite, scrambled eggs or chicken may be appreciated. By this stage you should divide her daily rations into two or maybe three meals, depending on how heavily in-whelp she is. The addition of a vitamin and mineral supplement should be given, following the manufacturer's instructions. This will safeguard against

WHELPING CHART

Served January	Due to Whelp March	Served February	Due to Whelp April	Served March	Due to Whelp May	Served April	Due to Whelp June	Served May	Due to Whelp July	Served June	Due to Whelp August	Served July	Due to Whelp September	Served August	Due to Whelp October	Served September	Due to Whelp November	Served October	Due to Whelp December	Served November	Due to Whelp January	Served December	Due to Whelp February
1	5	1	5	1	3	1	3	1	3	1	3	1	2	1	3	1	3	1	3	1	3	1	2
2	6	2	6	2	4	2	4	2	4	2	4	2	3	2	4	2	4	2	4	2	4	2	3
3	7	3	7	3	5	3	5	3	5	3	5	3	4	3	5	3	5	3	5	3	5	3	4
4	8	4	8	4	6	4	6	4	6	4	6	4	5	4	6	4	6	4	6	4	6	4	5
5	9	5	9	5	7	5	7	5	7	5	7	5	6	5	7	5	7	5	7	5	7	5	6
6	10	6	10	6	8	6	8	6	8	6	8	6	7	6	8	6	8	6	8	6	8	6	7
7	11	7	11	7	9	7	9	7	9	7	9	7	8	7	9	7	9	7	9	7	9	7	8
8	12	8	12	8	10	8	10	8	10	8	10	8	9	8	10	8	10	8	10	8	10	8	9
9	13	9	13	9	11	9	11	9	11	9	11	9	10	9	11	9	11	9	11	9	11	9	10
10	14	10	14	10	12	10	12	10	12	10	12	10	11	10	12	10	12	10	12	10	12	10	11
11	15	11	15	11	13	11	13	11	13	11	13	11	12	11	13	11	13	11	13	11	13	11	12
12	16	12	16	12	14	12	14	12	14	12	14	12	13	12	14	12	14	12	14	12	14	12	13
13	17	13	17	13	15	13	15	13	15	13	15	13	14	13	15	13	15	13	15	13	15	13	14
14	18	14	18	14	16	14	16	14	16	14	16	14	15	14	16	14	16	14	16	14	16	14	15
15	19	15	19	15	17	15	17	15	17	15	17	15	16	15	17	15	17	15	17	15	17	15	16
16	20	16	20	16	18	16	18	16	18	16	18	16	17	16	18	16	18	16	18	16	18	16	17
17	21	17	21	17	19	17	19	17	19	17	19	17	18	17	19	17	19	17	19	17	19	17	18
18	22	18	22	18	20	18	20	18	20	18	20	18	19	18	20	18	20	18	20	18	20	18	19
19	23	19	23	19	21	19	21	19	21	19	21	19	20	19	21	19	21	19	21	19	21	19	20
20	24	20	24	20	22	20	22	20	22	20	22	20	21	20	22	20	22	20	22	20	22	20	21
21	25	21	25	21	23	21	23	21	23	21	23	21	22	21	23	21	23	21	23	21	23	21	22
22	26	22	26	22	24	22	24	22	24	22	24	22	23	22	24	22	24	22	24	22	24	22	23
23	27	23	27	23	25	23	25	23	25	23	25	23	24	23	25	23	25	23	25	23	25	23	24
24	28	24	28	24	26	24	26	24	26	24	26	24	25	24	26	24	26	24	26	24	26	24	25
25	29	25	29	25	27	25	27	25	27	25	27	25	26	25	27	25	27	25	27	25	27	25	26
26	30	26	30	26	28	26	28	26	28	26	28	26	27	26	28	26	28	26	28	26	28	26	27
27	31	27	1 (MAY)	27	29	27	29	27	29	27	29	27	28	27	29	27	29	27	29	27	29	27	28
28	1 (APR.)	28	2	28	30	28	30	28	30	28	30	28	29	28	30	28	30	28	30	28	30	28	1 (MAR.)
29	2	29	3	29	31	29	1 (JULY)	29	31	29	31	29	30	29	31	29	1 (DEC.)	29	31	29	31	29	2
30	3			30	1 (JUNE)	30	2	30	1 (AUG.)	30	1 (SEP.)	30	1 (OCT.)	30	1 (NOV.)	30	2	30	1 (JAN.)	30	1 (FEB.)	30	3
31	4			31	2			31	2			31	2	31	2			31	2			31	4

Eclampsia and help the development of the puppies' bones and teeth. It is essential that she gets plenty of good food.

If the puppies are to be whelped in the house, you should prepare a room where she will not be disturbed by unwanted well-wishers. Chinese Cresteds are really not suited to being outside-kennel dogs; human companionship is very important to them, and they will not tolerate cold conditions. A bitch that is heavily in-whelp should not be left with any other dogs. All manner of accidents could happen while they are playing, and she will most probably become intolerant of them anyway. The average gestation time for all breeds is around sixty-three days, and Chinese Cresteds tend to whelp earlier rather than later. They can whelp any time from fifty-eight days, so be prepared in plenty of time. The bitch should have the chance to get used to her whelping box, although she may not be too interested to begin with. She may have different ideas for her nest, such as her favourite chair or even your bed. Before she is due to whelp, make sure you have the following items to hand:

Clean towels.
Antiseptic solution to wash your hands.
Hot-water bottle.
A suitable box for the newly-born puppies.
A pair of sterile round-ended scissors, in case it is necessary to cut umbilical cords.
Thread, already cut, to tie cords.
Kitchen roll to grip puppies if they need assistance coming into the world. They can be very slippery.
A box of tissues.

I have found that a closed-in whelping box is very successful for Chinese Cresteds. No extra heating is needed as the bitch's body heat is sufficient, once the door is closed. A D.I.Y. blanket box turned on its side makes an excellent whelping box, especially if it is plastic-coated, which makes cleaning so simple. A small modification to the lid to give a ventilation gap of about two inches at the top and a closing hook at each end is all that is required. This keeps the puppies in a warm, moist atmosphere and they thrive in their 'den'. Heat lamps tend to dry out puppies, and some bitches do not like the overhead heat. Draughts are

Pekevista Sum Chik Mei Of Kojak with a litter of five pups – Three Hairless and two Powderpuffs.

Kojak Kalypso with her four-day-old puppies – two Hairless and one Powderpuff: Itzcuintli Xquisite, Itzcuintli Xclusive and Itzcuintli Xcuseme.

always a problem, no matter how warm you keep the room. Many people like to use the electric heat pads which go under the bedding. I have to confess that I have never had the courage to try one, in case anything should go wrong.

I have found that the Vetbed type of bedding is ideal for whelping and nursing. It is warm, snug, and easily washed. If you use it on top of a layer of newspaper or an old sheet, urine and other fluids will soak through. There is therefore no need to disturb the bitch in order to change or clean the bedding between arrivals. It is also strong enough to withstand the bitch tugging or biting at it when nesting during labour. Remember to wash it when it is new to remove any loose fluff.

It is important to stay with your bitch, whatever the time of day she chooses to have her babies. (It will most probably be the middle of the night!) It will give her confidence, and you are on the spot if anything should go wrong. Anyway, it is always a moment never to be missed – the arrival of a new, tiny life.

If your bitch is a Powderpuff, her coat should be clipped underneath and around the tail. Crests and topknots should be tied up out of the way. If you decide against trimming the coat, you must be be prepared for a lot of extra work: care must be taken to ensure that the puppies do not get tangled in the hair. This also applies to the Hairless bitch: a single long hair from the tail will be sufficient to act as a tourniquet around the legs of a new-born pup. Fortunately, this is usually the only cause for concern, as Chinese Cresteds are free whelpers and make very good mothers.

At the start of labour, your bitch will become restless and this is often accompanied by shivering. She may still be reluctant to go into the whelping box, so you will need to keep a close eye on her at all times. Eventually, she will be ready to go into the whelping box, and she will start nesting. This consists of digging into, and tugging at her bedding. Once the bitch starts straining hard, the water bag will appear as a small, dark bubble. After a few more pushes, the puppy should appear. If nothing happens after an hour of straining, it is advisable to seek advice from your veterinary surgeon, as any further delay could prove disastrous. Always note the times of each new arrival. If your bitch appears calm, she may go as long as two hours between each delivery.

New-born puppies soon lose body heat, so keep the room very

Six-week-old puppies – two Hairless and one Powderpuff.

A Chinese Crested puppy pictured at eight weeks old. This was a very small pup.

warm and make sure they are thoroughly dried with a soft, clean towel, especially the Powderpuffs, who obviously take longer to dry. As soon as the membrane around the puppy is broken, use a tissue to gently wipe away any fluid and mucus from the nose and mouth. If the bitch is slow to break the membrane, tear it open yourself. A Hairless bitch may have difficulty severing the umbilical cord, if she has small, wide-spaced or missing teeth. This is a task that you must be prepared to take on, and it is surprising how thick and strong the cords can be. You will need to use round-ended sterilised scissors and cut close to the placenta, after pinching with the finger and thumb for a minute. The cord can also be tied off with a piece of thread. Many breeders do not like their bitches to eat the placentas as it causes diarrhoea. We allow our bitches to eat them if they want to. So long as no extra food is given for a few hours, other than a drink, no problem arises. Do make sure the placenta comes away in its entirety. If in any doubt, call your veterinary surgeon. He will give the bitch an injection to help her expel it.

As each new pup arrives, remove the others to a small box to prevent them from becoming wet again. Most bitches will not object to this, but watch out for any signs of distress. The bitch's well-being must be your top priority at this stage. The box for the new puppies should contain a warm hot-water bottle, well wrapped in a soft clean towel. Lay the puppies on this, and lightly cover them with a small towel. This will keep them safe and warm while the mother is attending to the new arrival. If she is taking her time between puppies they can be returned to her.

Occasionally a puppy will appear limp and lifeless after it has been released from its membrane. Do not panic. Wipe the nose and mouth clear of mucus and liquid and then rub firmly but gently with a towel. Hold the head pointing downwards, and at the same time gently squeeze and release the rib cage. Careful opening of the mouth can also get the puppy to gasp, and help it to start breathing. This should be done for several minutes, and you should be rewarded with a healthy puppy. After this traumatic start to life, let the pup rest in the warm box.

One of the many myths surrounding the Chinese Crested is that the Powderpuffs are born in order to keep their Hairless littermates warm. The origin of this story is a mystery, for the new-born Powderpuff's coat is no longer than that of any other new-born coated breed. It has hardly enough hair to keep itself warm, let alone its Hairless brothers and sisters. In a small litter there may not be a Powderpuff at all.

As soon as whelping is finished, the next and most important step is to make sure the puppies are suckling properly so that they take a good feed of colostrum. This is a sticky, highly digestible first milk, which is rich in protein and fats containing vital antibodies to give the puppies immunity for the first twelve weeks of life. If you spend time helping the puppies to feed at this stage, it may well save you from heartache and disappointment later on.

The average birth weight is around four to six ounces, and puppies should almost double this in their first week, if they are doing well. Some pups are born with dewclaws, and it is advisable to have the back dewclaws removed at three days old. Front dewclaws can also be removed at the same time. I leave front dewclaws on, for no other reason than that our first Chinese Crested, Cannybuff Christy, used hers as toothpicks!

After whelping, the bitch will need special attention. Her tail should be kept clean; it can get quite soiled and will become very sore if is not attended to. The best treatment is to bathe the tail with a mild antiseptic solution such as Savlon. The bitch must be given plenty of good food, at least three times a day, and a supply of clean water. If she will not drink water, warm diluted milk will usually be acceptable.

Bitches who normally cannot tolerate milk, seem able to thrive on it while they are feeding a litter. For the first three weeks, the bitch's intake of food can almost treble, if she has a large litter. You should also continue giving her the mineral supplement she was getting when she was in whelp.

The whelping box must be kept scrupulously clean, so the bedding should be changed regularly. Check that the puppies are suckling all the teats. If any should appear hard, gently draw some milk off and get a puppy to have a good feed from it. This problem usually arises with a small litter. Puppies tend to have their favourite spot, and the not so popular teats can be neglected, which can cause the bitch much discomfort. The kneading action of puppies stimulates the bitch's milk flow, but make sure that you trim their nails once a week. They grow very quickly and can easily scratch the bitch at feeding time.

WEANING

Puppies can be weaned on to any good puppy food from three weeks onwards, if they are ready. In recent years some excellent products have been developed which take the hit-and-miss out of weaning and puppy feeding. As a result, the problem of upset tummies, caused by too much meat in the diet, rarely occurs. If the bitch has plenty of milk, and she is enjoying her babies, there is no need to rush weaning. Some people worry if the litter is not totally weaned by five weeks. Many bitches regurgitate their food for their pups, and this should not be frowned upon. It is, after all, nature's way.

Rice pudding and human baby foods are not really the right diet for dogs, even if they are enjoyed. It is important to give a good, balanced diet right from the start, as this will strengthen teeth and bones. Do not over-do the vitamin and mineral supplements; excess dosage can do more harm than good. I have found that weaning puppies as naturally as possible produces healthy animals, with no tummy upsets. Their bodies are firm, rather than being floppy and overweight. When the puppies are fully weaned and mother's milk has dried up, do not be tempted to give cow's milk. It is difficult to digest and often results in diarrhoea and spots on the puppies' skins. Fresh water should be available at all times.

Ch. Itzcuintli Xquisite at nine months.

Itzcuintli Xcuseme at nine months.

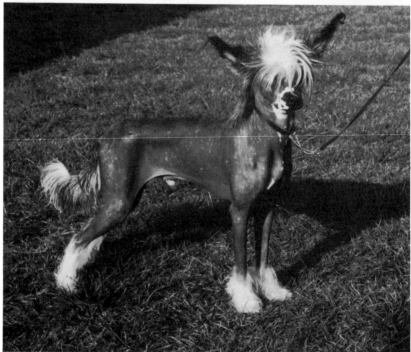

Chapter Ten

SELECTING AND
CARING FOR A PUPPY

As soon as a Chinese Crested puppy has been born, you can judge its potential by looking at its conformation. The length of neck, shoulder placement, hind angulation and rib cage can all be assessed. Chinese Cresteds do not change as much during development as some other breeds. The Chinese Crested conforms to the 'classic' dog conformation, and is not developed from other differently shaped breeds. As a result, there are not so many things that can go wrong.

The new-born puppy's skull is almost twice the length of the foreface – this will lengthen as the puppy matures. With experience, you will be able to judge which puppy's head will develop the elegant balance and fine chiselling that is typical of the best Crested head. A rule of thumb is that the head should not look coarse at this stage. The coat pattern of the Hairless is easily defined. The crest looks like a little silken cap, and minute hairs on the feet and tail are clearly visible. The density of the hairs will give you a good idea of whether the crest, socks and plume

*Ch Kojak
Kavalkade at
eight weeks.*

*Ch. Kojak
Kavalkade at
two years.*

Pearce.

will be full or sparse at maturity. Any excess hair will obviously be visible. The colour of the hair does vary at birth. It can be white or almost black, which grows through to white by around four months. A Powderpuff that is born black may well undergo the same colour change, ending up cream or white by the time it reaches maturity. Occasionally, Chinese Cresteds have black crests, but it is not very common. At this stage, the skin of the Hairless is quite shiny and it is very soft.

If you are buying a puppy, you may not have seen the litter at this early age. The pups will probably be between five and eight weeks when you first see them. At this stage, it should be quite easy to see which ones are the best. They should all be lively and inquisitive; if there is a shrinking violet, it will probably stay that way. Look for the dominant pups who move around proudly, investigating anything unusual, showing a promise of ring presence. The feet should be pointing straight forward, turning neither in nor out. There should be no signs of cow hocks or being out at the elbows. Ears, however, may or may not be erect in the Hairless. This is a variable factor, and it may take some time before the ear carriage finally settles. During teething, in particular, ears can do all manner of things; going up and down by the day. The puppy's expression is important, and I like to see a pup looking bright and lively. Don't be embarrassed to ask the breeder if you can look at the puppies' mouths. Even if all the teeth are not through in the Hairless, they will show as lumps in the gums, if they are to appear. Some Hairless do not get their teeth for quite a few weeks. However, if you can see both parents, it will give you more idea of what to expect. The breeder should be willing to advise you, especially if you intend to show the puppy.

Watch the puppy when it is moving naturally. Faults such as cow hocks, poor fronts, weak quarters and top-lines rarely improve. Equally, any indication of an under-shot or excessively over-shot mouth, should be regarded with suspicion. Check that a male puppy is entire; this can be seen at a very early age with this breed. In my experience, a well-bred, good-looking eight-week-old Crested puppy that has been well reared, should fulfil its potential. The only thing difficult to predict is its final size, which is a problem in most breeds. The smallest puppy in the litter at birth does not always turn out to be the smallest, when all

*Ch. Kojak Kryspar at
eight weeks (left) and
at six months (above).*

*Ch. Kojak
Kryspar at
two years.*

Pearce.

the pups reach maturity. Bloodlines have an influence on when the puppies finish growing; so be advised by the breeder. It is a good idea to weigh puppies regularly from birth. Over the years you will be able to tell which will end up too large, or too small.

Puppies usually change home at around eight to ten weeks, and this can be a traumatic experience. In order to make the transition as smooth as possible, keep to the diet given by the breeder, until the puppy has settled in to its new home. Then if you intend to change the puppy's food, do it gradually. If you already have an older dog, it may well prove to be an excellent guardian, and allow the newcomer to sleep with it. This can be a real advantage: it stops the puppy feeling anxious and the new owner is also spared some sleepless nights!

CARE OF THE YOUNG CHINESE CRESTED PUPPY

Puppies should be wormed for roundworms at three to four weeks, and then again at seven weeks. Every care should be taken to follow the manufacturer's instructions as to weight and dosage. Nearly all puppies have roundworms, and for this reason, children should never be allowed to play with young puppies, however scrupulously clean you may keep them.

Chinese Crested puppies are extremely agile and are capable of climbing over mother's back at just a few hours old. This agility can be a problem; most youngsters will make easy work of the average wire-mesh puppy run. Their feet are almost prehensile, and they will be able to climb right to the top. Obviously, this cannot be allowed to happen, for their own safety. Even if you cover the run with a roof of mesh, the pups may still climb along like trapeze artists! The answer to this problem is not to have a wire-mesh run at all. The alternative is to have one made of plastic-coated board, at least eighteen inches high. This has the added advantage of being easy to clean.

Do not be surprised if the Hairless puppies are still without their milk teeth at seven weeks old. This may be the reason why bitches are happy to feed these pups for a longer period, while often turning the Powderpuffs away – although most bitches will probably prefer to leave the litter at night, as soon as they are a few weeks old.

There are numerous puppy foods available on the market, and

whether you decide to feed fresh, cooked, tinned or a complete diet, the object remains the same. The aim is to encourage the development of healthy, active youngsters. Their play often appears rough, but no harm is done. The pups appreciate plenty of toys, and they love to have large biscuits to chew. By the time they are six to seven weeks old, the pups should be eating at least four meals a day. Many breeders like to give cereal feeds, as well as meat and biscuit. We have found, over the years, that Chinese Cresteds develop far better if you do not feed separate cereal meals at all. There is sufficient nourishment in their puppy meal or complete diet.

Vaccinations usually begin at twelve weeks, when the puppy's natural immunity has diminished. A further dose will be needed at fourteen or sixteen weeks, depending on your veterinary surgeon's recommendation. The vaccines used today are for four main diseases: distemper, leptospirosis, hepatitis and parvovirus. Occasionally, a puppy will react to the vaccine and develop slight diarrhoea. Keep a check on this, as puppies can become ill and dehydrated very quickly.

The four daily meals will gradually reduce to one meal a day when the puppy is fully grown. During the winter it is advisable to introduce an extra meal to prevent weight loss. It is advisable to keep a close check on the puppy's teeth when the milk teeth are being shed. Milk teeth, especially the canines, are often reluctant to come away, even when the adult teeth are through. This will result in a double set of teeth, and the milk teeth will need to be removed by your veterinary surgeon, otherwise the dog's mouth will be spoiled for good.

Chapter Eleven

CARE OF THE ADULT CHINESE CRESTED

A well-balanced diet, coupled with regular exercise are the essential elements needed to keep a dog healthy and in good condition. There is a huge range of prepared foods available for dogs. Whatever diet you choose to feed – fresh, tinned or frozen meat, or the more convenient complete diets – the food must be of good quality. Everyone has their own particular method of feeding their dogs, and we are very fortunate to have such a huge selection to choose from.

One thing I have discovered is that feeds without maize and added dried milk seem to suit Chinese Cresteds better. Some dogs react to foods with a high preservative content, so careful observation is needed to ensure that you are not, unknowingly, putting your dog in danger. I had this experience when one of our own dogs reacted to some pre-cooked food with added preservative. We had to call in the vet, and the dog was unwell for several days. Cow's milk has been found to aggravate the spotty condition in some 'teenage' Cresteds. Ideally, substitute milk should not be given to dogs, as they are unable to digest

*Finnish Ch.
Kojak Kordier
dressed for
winter.*

*Kojak
Kontribution
relaxing at home.*

lactose (milk sugar) as they mature, and this can cause diarrhoea.

A Chinese Crested that is in good condition should have its rib cage nicely covered, a slight tuck-up of the abdomen, and hip bones just under the surface – they should not protrude, like those of the Afghan Hound. If, on the other hand, the hip bones have completely vanished, it is a sure sign that the dog is overweight. It is surprising how much food a Chinese Crested requires to maintain the correct weight. As with most breeds, some dogs are very greedy, and others can be finicky. One of the breed's peculiarities is the Chinese Crested's love of fruit and all kinds of raw vegetables. Apples and pears seem to be particular favourites, followed closely by grapes, peaches, bananas, strawberries and even oranges. A dog will delicately eat an apple core and leave the pips in a neat pile when it has finished.

The Chinese Crested is an easy breed to care for on a day-to-day basis. The Breed Standard states that nails should be long, but they still need to be trimmed regularly. The typical extended toes and hare feet of the Chinese Crested mean that the nails do not wear down as quickly as those of a dog with round, tight cat-feet. The quicks are long, so it is relatively easy to trim and leave the required length of nail. Care of teeth is of the utmost importance. Puppies should get used to having their teeth cleaned with a junior-size toothbrush. If you have a dog with good teeth, it would be a great shame to lose them through neglect.

The Hairless variety love to sunbathe, and in the summer months it is a good idea to rub a little baby lotion or moisturiser into the dog's skin. Whole colours are not such a problem, but extra care must be taken with the spotteds and poorly pigmented dogs. The pink skin has no melanin, and so it will burn very quickly. A barrier sun cream is very useful, and is a must in warmer climates. Bedding should be kept scrupulously clean. In the summer, cotton bedding is preferable as it stops the Hairless getting too warm and sticky, a condition which can lead to skin rashes. A Hairless achieves its full colour in the summer, and this fades in the winter. If you are lucky enough to have a south-facing conservatory, it will make an ideal sun lounge on sunny winter days, and your dogs will not lose too much colour. Occasionally, Hairless Chinese Cresteds develop black-heads and/or white-heads. The black-heads are not so apparent in the darker-coloured dogs, but it can be quite unsightly in the

Int. Ch Highclass Mr Ching Lee of Aes, pictured at eight years old.

The Chinese Crested always forms a special relationship with its owner.

mahogany and spotteds. On the whole, the marks referred to as black-heads are, in fact, dead incomplete hairs just above the surface of the skin. These can be removed quite easily with a pair of fine tweezers – if you can bear it! Clean the skin afterwards with a gentle antiseptic cream or solution. This should be the end of the problem, but occasionally the area will become infected. All dogs are different, and some may have allergies to different things. I have heard of some breeders who have found that their Hairless dogs react to wool, though I have not found this in my own dogs. The best advice I can give is to be aware of your dog's daily health and condition, and take appropriate action when necessary.

Many believe that because the Chinese Crested is a hardy breed, the Hairless will not need a coat in winter. In fact, they are happy to play outside in the cold for a short while. But if they are taken for a walk in the winter, they will need a coat. After all, there are very few humans who would like to go out in the cold without their clothes. I have found that a simple, knitted body stocking keeps the dogs snug and warm, without constricting their movement. One of the myths surrounding the Chinese Crested is that they have a higher body temperature than other dogs, in order to compensate for their lack of coat. The temperature of the average dog is four degrees higher than that of humans, so maybe that is where the confusion originates. The Hairless certainly feel very warm to the touch, but their temperature is around 101.5 degrees Farenheit, which is that of all dogs. It is always a good idea to be aware of an individual dog's normal temperature, as there is usually a small deviation from the normal in both dogs and humans. If you know what is normal for your dog, it will be a help if it is taken ill at any time.

Generally speaking, the breed is healthy and hardy, and with proper care and lots of love and attention, you will be rewarded with a very special blend of affection and companionship that is one of the most endearing facets of the Chinese Crested.

CARE OF THE ELDERLY CHINESE CRESTED

Barring tragic accidents or illness, you should expect to enjoy the company of your Chinese Crested for many years. They usually live to a reasonable age, and I have known some that have reached the grand old age of 15 years or more. An elderly dog needs just as much care and attention as it did when it was a puppy, if not more. If it has been a show dog and has lived with a group, it will enjoy some extra spoiling as it gets older. In fact, it may be advisable to take it away from the group as it loses its place in the pecking order to a younger dog. This is to make sure that no bullying takes place, as this can make the veteran's life a misery.

An elderly dog will obviously not exercise as energetically as it did when it was young. Weight will therefore have to be watched, especially if there are signs of stiffness in the joints and muscles. Reduced exercise will also mean that nails are not worn down so quickly, and they will need trimming more regularly. The elderly Hairless will appreciate a coat to keep it warm when it is outside. Teeth can cause problems, and any teeth that are left should be inspected regularly in case they cause the gums to become infected, which would be very painful.

When life is no longer a pleasure for the elderly dog, it is unkind to prolong it, especially if pain is involved. It is always heartbreaking to lose an old friend, and, to begin with, there is a terrible void in your life. However, you always have the memories to treasure, and, in time, a new puppy can eventually fill the gap – and the fun and enjoyment of owning a dog starts all over again.

Chapter Twelve

DIGESTION

Digestion is the process which breaks down large food constituents into forms that can be absorbed by the intestinal tract of the body, which is comparatively short in the dog. This breakdown is achieved by chewing, mixing and transporting the mixture through the digestive canal. Dogs eat quickly and only hard pieces of food are chewed. The majority is bolted down in large lumps, which is quite normal, and Chinese Cresteds are no exception.

Digestion begins in the stomach. The dog's digestive juices have a high level of hydrochloric acid which together with the enzyme pepsin prepares proteins for further breakdown in the small intestine. Fats and carbohydrates are not broken down in the stomach. Secretions lower the acidity of the mixture before it passes from the stomach into the small intestine via the duodenum and meets enzymes from the pancreas. Bile is secreted through the bile duct from the liver and is important in the digestion of fats and the absorption of fatty acids.

Proteins of animal origin are digested more readily than those from plants. Approximately 90 per cent of fats are digested, and it is important that starches, in the form of cereals, are well

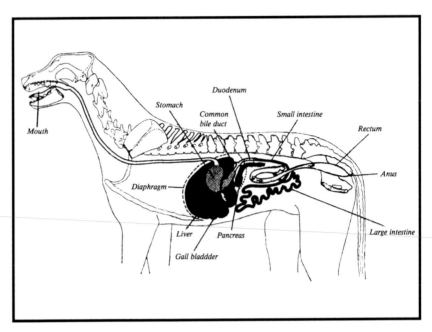

cooked as their digestibility varies considerably. Some dogs also find difficulty in dealing with lactose (milk sugar), except in early puppyhood.

Older animals lack the enzyme lactase. We have found that this intolerance of milk could contribute to the 'spotty problems' of many young Chinese Cresteds. Giving no milk after weaning certainly reduces the incidence of spots. Excessive amounts of poorly cooked starch and/or lactose can cause diarrhoea. Minerals, vitamins and trace elements are mainly absorbed in the small intestine. The normal digestion of fats is necessary for the absorption of the fat soluble vitamins A, D, E and K.

The dog's digestion is mainly completed in the small intestine where the digested material is absorbed into the bloodstream and lymphatic system. The bulk of the water is also absorbed here. The efficient function of the large intestine is of great importance for the water balance of the dog, and in the formation of well-formed faeces. Undigested material from a poor-quality diet can impair the health and well-being of the dog. A good diet and efficient digestion is the only way the dog can be supplied with the energy sources and nutrients it requires for growth, health and reproduction. Clean water is also important, and this should be available at all times.

VITAMINS

It should be not be necessary to supplement a balanced manufactured dog food with extra vitamins and minerals. In fact, it may prove harmful. Vitamins function in the enzyme systems in individual cells and are involved in the utilisation of other nutrients. A deficiency in vitamin intake can result in diseases and various other problems. They do not provide calories, nor do they become component parts of bone, muscle, blood or nerves. They can be divided into two groups: fat-soluble and water-soluble.

FAT-SOLUBLE VITAMINS:

VITAMIN A: This is vital in the production and maintenance of skin, mucous membranes and skeletal components. It is well-known for its role in the maintenance of the retina of the eye and night vision. A deficiency of vitamin A will cause loss of appetite and skin lesions. An excess is as harmful as a deficiency, as it can cause a crippling bone disease. Fish liver oils are a good source of vitamin A.

VITAMIN D: This plays a very important part in the absorption of calcium from the intestine, and depositing calcium and phosphorus salts in bones and teeth. A deficiency of vitamin D in puppies will result in malformed bones, commonly known as rickets. An excess of vitamin D and calcium encourages early ossification and deforms bones. It will also cause extensive calcification of the lungs, kidneys and stomach.

VITAMIN E: This is important in maintaining the stability of cell membranes. Various abnormalities result from a deficiency, including muscular weakness and reproductive problems. Vitamin E is found in vegetable seeds e.g. wheat, maize, rape, sunflower, soya beans, and it is extracted from the oils.

VITAMIN K: This stimulates the production of thrombin, the constituent required for clotting blood. In the dog it is synthesised by intestinal bacteria, therefore there should be no deficiency in a healthy dog.

WATER-SOLUBLE VITAMINS:

VITAMIN C: This is known as ascorbic acid, and it is not considered essential in a dog's diet. As with Vitamin K, it is synthesised in the dog's intestine.

VITAMIN Bl: This is known as thiamin, and it is involved in carbohydrate metabolism. A deficiency will result in loss of appetite and inadequate gastric secretions. In humans a thiamin deficiency is known as beriberi. Vitamin Bl is found naturally in yeast, cereals and vegetables .

VITAMIN B2: This is known as riboflavin, and its major task is in fat and protein metabolism. A deficiency may result in slow or interrupted growth in puppies, loss of weight in adults, loss of appetite, mild anaemia and dermatitis. It is found in cereals, animal by-products and brewer's yeast.

PANTOTHENIC ACID: This is another member of the Vitamin B complex, and it works in enzyme systems involved in carbohydrate, fat and protein metabolism. A deficiency can result in slow growth, loss of hair, gastro-intestinal ulcers and a reduced resistance to virus infection. Pantothenic acid is found in wheat middlings and brewer's yeast.

NICOTINIC ACID (niacin): This plays a vital role in carbohydrate and fat metabolism. It also helps in the conversion of Vitamin A into a form required for night vision. A deficiency may show itself in the form of sores on the tongue and lining of the mouth, known as pellagra in man. A rich source of nicotinic acid is found in brewer's yeast and animal protein.

FOLIC ACID: This is primarily involved in the formation of red blood cells in the bone marrow. A deficiency will result in anaemia. Although added to food by manufacturers, it is produced in the small intestine.

BIOTIN: This is involved in energy and protein metabolism. Sulpha drugs taken orally can produce a deficiency as they kill the organisms which synthesise biotin in the intestine. Feeding raw egg-whites can have a similar effect. The protein avidin in raw egg-white reacts with the biotin to make it inactive.

CHOLINE: This is synthesised by the body, so long as good quality protein is fed. A deficiency results in fat accumulating in the liver, resulting in impaired liver function.

VITAMIN B12: This is involved in fat and carbohydrate metabolism and the synthesis of myelin, which is a constituent of nerve tissue. It is well-known for its role in preventing pernicious anaemia in humans.

Supplementing extra vitamins, minerals and trace elements that are necessary to the dog's diet, can do more harm than good. Excessive intake of the fat-soluble vitamins A, D, E and K will result in storage in the body. An excess of the water-soluble B-complex and C vitamins will simply be excreted in the urine.

In this chapter I have tried to simplify a very complex and interesting subject to show the importance of correct balanced feeding for the good health of our dogs, who depend on their owners for their diet and well-being.

Chapter Thirteen

IN THE SHOW RING

The Hairless and Powderpuff are shown together in the same ring in Britain, a procedure which was adopted when The Kennel Club recognised the Powderpuff for exhibition in 1981. After recognition some judges were still reluctant to place a Powderpuff, however worthy, as they were not mentioned in the Interim Standard. At this stage the Chinese Crested was still classed as a rare breed, and did not qualify for Challenge Certificates. The breed was given Championship status in 1982, and the Revised Standard was finally issued in July 1984. Both varieties were then able to compete together, with no further problems regarding the Standard. However, this was not to be the end of the controversy which has blighted the breed for so many years. A move was made to separate the two varieties in the show ring, without success to date. Unfortunately, there will always be exhibitors and judges who feel it is impossible to judge the two varieties together. This should not really pose a problem. The significant differences are ear carriage, dentition and coat. The dog underneath is exactly the same. There will be differences in type, but that is for the judge to sort out. If judges find difficulty judging Hairless and Coated dogs of the same breed, how do they manage with Variety Classes or Best In Show, which feature many different breeds, some with long coats and others with short, smooth coats? In the arguments for separating the Hairless and Powderpuff, it is often quoted that the two varieties are shown separately in America. In fact, the American system is totally different, and although Powderpuffs and Hairless are separated in the show ring, the two varieties are inter-bred.

If the different breed varieties are separated by The Kennel Club, such as the Smooth and Long Coat Chihuahua, and the Rough and Smooth Collie, separate Challenge Certificates are awarded for each new breed that is created. After a certain interval of time inter-breeding of the two separated breeds is prohibited. The theory is that eventually each variety will breed true to type, and inter-breeding will not be necessary. The Chinese Crested is a unique breed in the world of show dogs. It is made up of two genetically inseparable varieties. Powderpuffs will always be produced from Hairless-to-Hairless matings, as well as from Hairless to Powderpuff matings. The Powderpuff cannot be bred out, however hard you may try. The result of separating the two varieties would be that Powderpuffs from these matings could not be registered. We would then have gone full circle, and they would be discarded once again. As a breed, the Chinese Crested has only a small gene bank to draw from; we therefore cannot afford to lose good stock just to pander to the whims of a few.

PREPARATION FOR THE SHOW RING

Preparing the Chinese Crested for the show ring is comparatively easy, and not so time-consuming as is the case in some breeds. The first step is to start training the young puppy to stand on a table, making it a game. Youngsters soon become bored, so don't over-do it – little and often is the best way. As a breed the Chinese Crested can be quite obstinate when it comes to lead-training, so all your patience may be needed here. As soon as your pup has completed its course of vaccinations, it is a good idea to join a dog-training club, which holds a ring craft class. There is usually one in most areas, which meets every week. The atmosphere is very friendly, and if you are new to showing, the instructor will be only too happy help and advise.

Show dogs always look more impressive if they free-stand away from the handler, and then move off on a loose lead. Unfortunately, not all dogs will oblige, and this can lead to difficulties. There are no Kennel Club rules on how to show dogs, except for prohibiting double handling from outside the ring. It is most important to remember that you will have only a few minutes to get the best out of your dog when you are in the show ring. If you need to stack the dog, you will not be penalised. I have found that puppies who need stacking often grow in confidence as they mature, and no longer need so much assistance.

HAIRLESS:

The health and quality of the dog's skin will depend entirely on your husbandry and feeding. The Chinese Crested must be fed properly and kept clean. A few spots may appear, however careful you are, particularly before the start of a season in bitches. The Hairless variety all have hair on their faces in varying amounts. It can be left, but most dogs look much nicer with clean faces, showing off the fine chiselling of the foreface. The easiest way to remove surplus hair is to use a small razor taking a line from the outer corner of the eye to the ear. Obviously, great care is needed. Stray hairs on the body can be removed in the same way. A little baby lotion or moisturiser after the pre-show bath will improve the appearance of the skin, if it is dry.

POWDERPUFF:

The foreface can be clipped in the same style as the Poodle. If this is done a few days before the show, a more natural look will be achieved. It is not compulsory to do this; the hair can be left to grow naturally. If you decide to clip the foreface, use a 10mm clipper head, taking a line from the outer corner of the eye to the ear. Never go above the eye-line. Clip a gentle curve from the ears to the 'Adam's apple', and do not go below it. The idea is to make the face look natural and not overdone. It will not make a short neck look longer. A small inverted 'v' can be scissored between the eyes to give a professional finish. Try not to put a parting down the centre of the topline. Powderpuff should look as natural as possible, although a parting may be necessary for dogs with a thick unruly coat.

Both varieties should be bathed the day before the show, with a good quality shampoo. The Powderpuff may benefit from having a conditioner added. This is usually the best time to clean the teeth, with a junior-size toothbrush. For the Powderpuff, the best results are always achieved by using a professional hair-drier, which blows deeply into the coat while you brush and tease out any knots. You will also need to tidy any thick hair from around the pads, and nails will need to be clipped. When the dog is completely dry, tie up the top-knot to keep hair out of the dog's eyes. If the coat has been groomed thoroughly and all knots removed, there will be very little to do on the the day of the show. The top-knot should be untied, and then brush right through the coat, finishing with a gentle combing with a wide-toothed comb.

Chapter Fourteen

JUDGING

It is not my intention to teach judges how to judge, but, as I have stressed throughout this book, the Chinese Crested has certain unique characteristics. It is therefore essential that judges are aware of these points in order to make a fair assessment in the show ring. It should always be remembered that judging is the most controversial area of the dog world. I believe that judging is an acquired art, which is developed over many years. However, you should never lose sight of the fact that in the end, the final result comes down to one person's opinion.

I have now been judging Chinese Crested for some ten years, and when I started exhibiting dogs, twenty-one years ago, the general practice was to serve an 'apprenticeship' before embarking on a judging career. It used to be very unusual to receive an invitation to judge within five years of starting in a breed. During this time it was assumed that you would have studied the breed, possibly bred some decent types, and, hopefully, developed an eye for a good dog – something some people never achieve. Many people begin judging before they have acquired a comprehensive knowledge of the breed. Their first classes often come at the end of a package of breeds, with the Chinese Crested almost treated as a "filler". This, I believe, is a great mistake. There is certainly no substitute for experience, and all serious judges should be prepared to serve their time, looking at as many dogs as possible and learning all they can about their chosen breed.

There are a few maxims that are important to remember when you start on a judging career. Always remember, it is an honour to be invited to judge, and when you are in the show ring it is the dogs who are the most important – not the judge. There is no place for prima donnas, or for settling old scores. It is the duty of every judge to ensure that he or she gives no favours and is not swayed by a previous judge's opinion. Do not allow yourself to be intimidated by over-zealous exhibitors. Ignore their attempts to thrust their dog forward, but remain polite at all times. Many of the dogs and the exhibitors may be known to you. The best attitude to adopt is to forget all you know of their reputations and judge the dogs, as you find them, on the day.

Take all possible care when you are going over the dogs. There is no excuse for heavy handling; after all, the dog does not belong to you. Always give puppies special consideration, and a little extra time if they are apprehensive. Some pups will still be teething, and so their mouths could be sensitive. The exhibitor could also be a novice, and judges should make allowances for nerves. All judges develop their own method of going over a dog. I have found that memory is the most essential requirement. It is vital to memorise how each dog impressed you, or failed to impress you. If you rely on making notes it can cause a lot of confusion when it comes to judging the class. In most cases, it is a complete waste of time, and the sight of a judge fumbling through notes does not give the exhibitors much confidence.

The most worrying comment that I hear from judges of all levels is that they find it impossible to assess the two varieties of Chinese Crested in the same class. Yet these people are often up-and-coming all-rounders, who regularly judge variety classes of mixed breeds. Even worse, some of them consider the two varieties to be two completely separate breeds. I seriously believe that if you have difficulty in accepting the unique characteristics of the ancient hairless breeds, you should decline any further invitations to judge. It is not fair on the exhibitors, and it is certainly detrimental to the breed. If you regularly judge variety classes, you should find absolutely no difficulty in assessing the two varieties of Chinese Crested. Obviously, quality and type (deer and cobby) does vary between the varieties, as it does within each variety. However, this does not make the task of assessing the Hairlesss and Powderpuff impossible, if you are a competent judge with full knowledge of the breed.

As with many toy breeds, Chinese Cresteds do not like to be handled on the floor or stared at through sunglasses. Hats and jangling bracelets can also be off-putting. Many dogs will also back away from smokers if they are not used to the smell. It is asking enough of a dog to be handled by a stranger, so don't do anything to worsen the situation for a potentially sensitive dog. Occasionally, judges will make odd noises in order to get the dogs to lift and use their ears. If this is done with Chinese Cresteds, it could have the opposite effect, as they often pull their ears back to unusual sights and sounds. It is far better to assess the dog while you have its complete attention on the table, and while it is moving individually.

If the weather is inclement, exhibitors would very much prefer to be judged under cover, if it is possible. A cold wind is very disturbing for the Hairless variety, and even those with the best toplines will arch their backs and look very sorry for themselves. If it is impossible to judge inside, try moving the dogs as much as possible. Luckily, we do have many caring and considerate judges who do just that.

Never worry about your next entry when you are judging. If it turns out that your top winners come from one kennel or blood-line, then so be it. The best dog must always go up, whoever it belongs to. A knowledgeable, pleasant, honest and decisive judge will have the respect of exhibitors, and will always attract a good entry.

Chapter Fifteen

THE FUTURE

The Chinese Crested is now well established both as a show dog, and as a delightful extrovert, affectionate companion. A marked improvement in quality and soundness has taken place over the last ten years, thanks to a few knowledgeable and dedicated breeders. The breed is no longer looked on as a joke in the show ring, and many successful owners of other breeds have joined the ranks of Crested lovers. In time, the knowledge and skills of these people will prove beneficial to the breed. The responsibility to further this improvement lies with both the breeders and judges. It is imperative to breed more selectively, and not to be content with mediocrity. I also believe that more courageous judging would do the breed a power of good. Far too many judges forgive basic unsoundness in the breed, and this can only cause harm in the long run. There is nothing worse than the sight of poor movement, which accompanies pinched fronts, cow hocks, barrel chests, and dogs out at the elbows. Poor mouths are also a subject of much contention. The Chinese Crested has a basically simple conformation, and so there is no excuse for incompetent judging.

There is no doubt that the Hairless-Powderpuff debate will

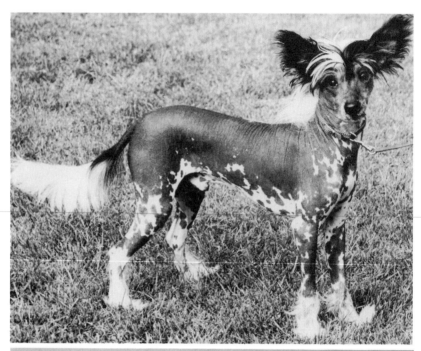

The Hairless and Powderpuff, typifying the unique characteristics of the Chinese Crested.

John Darby

continue to rage within the breed. All manner of changes to the Standard regarding drop or erect ears in the Powderpuff will not alter the fact that Powderpuffs' ears are predominantly dropped. Stripping and taping the ears proves nothing; Powderpuff pups will still be born with drop ears. This unique breed has two varieties, that is a fact of life. We should all feel privileged to be involved with such a delightful breed. It is our responsibility to conserve the Chinese Crested for the enjoyment of future generations. International cooperation between knowledgeable and dedicated breeders is probably the best way forward. I have made many friends throughout the world, all dedicated to improving the breed, and frustrated by the interference of a few. It is not a breed for the novice to embark on. Equally, if you cannot cope with the unique features of the Chinese Crested, this is not the breed for you. The Chinese Crested has survived, true to type, for many centuries, and I am sure it will continue to thrive, now that it has so many devotees.

Staround
Atlanta

Chapter Sixteen

BEST OF THE FOUNDATION STOCK

STAROUND ATLANTA
Whelped: 2-8-1968
Colour: Blue
Breeder: Mrs Ruth Harris
Owner: Mrs Dorothy Tyler

			Palo of Cresthaven
		Inco of Cresthaven	
	Intoo of Cresthaven (Spotted dog weight around 11lb)		Snowflake
		Milya of Cresthaven	Mr Softie of Cresthaven
			Sugar of Cresthaven
Staround Atlanta			Tuno of Cresthaven
		Navo of Cresthaven	
	Alto of Cresthaven (Mahogany weight around 10lb)		Trixie of Cresthaven
		Efta of Cresthaven	Gold Boy of Cresthaven
			Milya of Cresthaven

A member of one of the first two litters bred and reared by Ruth Harris. Sparse Crested, lovely skin and long hare feet.

*Staround
Himalaya*

STAROUND HIMALAYA

Whelped: 12-4-1974
Colour: Blue
Breeder: Mrs Ruth Harris
Owner: Mrs Dorothy Tyler

			Staround Ahn Ahn Lee
		Staround Koko	
	Staround Voo Doo		Sobesta of Cresthaven
			Staround Arko
		Staround Lhaza	
Staround Himalaya			Staround Lily Lee
			Lee Chee Lee
		Staround Ahn Ahn Lee	
	Staround Nyssa		Chi Chi Lee
			Nero of Cresthaven
		Staround China Princess	
			Alto of Cresthaven

A bitch of lovely type. An offer of £1,200 was made for her at one point in her show career. Note the 'lacing' on her legs.

*Staround
Tyla*

STAROUND TYLA
Whelped: 19-8-1972
Colour: Blue
Breeder: Mrs Ruth Harris
Owner: Mrs Dorothy Tyler

				Fu Manchu Lee
			Lee Chee Lee	
				Chu Chin Chow
		Staround Ahn Ahn Lee		
				Chung Lee
			Chi Chi Lee	
				Blinkey
Staround Tyla				
				Marbo of Cresthaven
			Nero of Cresthaven	
				Fuzzy of Cresthaven
		Staround Brittania		
				Justo of Cresthaven
			Sobesta of Cresthaven	
				Pow'na of Cresthaven

The epitome of the Standard; beautifully balanced, with a level topline. This was the bitch that first attracted me to the breed, and was always a great favourite.

STAROUND QUANTO
Whelped: 10-2-1977
Colour: Blue
Breeder: Mrs Ruth Harris
Owner: Mrs Mary Smith

			Lee Chee Lee
		Staround Ahn Ahn Lee	Chi Chi Lee
	Staround Koko		Justo of Cresthaven
		Sobesta of Cresthaven	I'ow Na of Cresthaven
Staround Quanto			Lee Chee Lee
		Staround Ahn Ahn Lee	Chi Chi Lee
	Staround Hunta		
		Staround China Princess	Nero of Cresthaven
			Alto of Cresthaven

This dog dominated the show ring in the early days and was unlucky to be born before Challenge Certificates were allocated. A well-balanced dog with an excellent crest and plume.

CANNYBUFF CILVA

Whelped: 8-8-1975
Colour: Blue
Breeder: Mrs Crowther-Davies
Owner:

		Staround Apollo
	Staround Expo	
		Staround China Princess
Cannybuff Cilva		
		Staround Koko
	Staround Channa	
		Staround Lhaza

One of the best from the Cannybuff Kennel. His outstanding features were a straight front, balanced head and a lovely skin.

*Winterlea
Intoo Aes*

WINTERLEA INTOO AES
Whelped: 2-2-1977
Colour: Pale Mahogany
Breeder: Mrs Margorie Mooney
Owner: Mrs Olwyn Harbottle

		Horn of Cresthaven	Justo of Cresthaven
	Ming Li of Winterlea		Noga of Cresthaven
		Winterlea Inza of Cresthaven	Inco of Cresthaven
Winterlea Intoo Aes			Milya of Cresthaven
		Ming Li of Winterlea	Horn of Cresthaven
	Winterlea Sunbelle		Winterlea Inza of Cresthaven
		Heathermount Quo Vadis	Winterlea Starba of Cresthaven

An extremely glamourous little dog, who sired the first UK champion dog – Aes Into Dynasty. Sound throughout with good head and expression; superb movement.

Chapter Seventeen

THE CHAMPIONS

BRITISH

CHAMPION. AES INTO DYNASTY. (J.W.)

Whelped: May 1979
Colour: Mahogany
Breeder: Mrs Olwyn Harbottle

Ch Aes Into Dynasty	Winterlea Intoo Aes	Ming Li of Winterlea	Horn of Cresthaven
			Winterlea Inza Of Crest Haven
		Winterlea Sunbelle	Ming Li Of Winterlea
			Heathermount Quo Vadis
	Cresta of Capilon (Powderpuff)	Staround Quanto	Staround Koko
			Staround Hunta
		Clogheen Natasha	Staround Quanto
			Staround Irma

The dog who really made breed history. He was the first UK Champion, gaining his three CCs at three consecutive shows in 1982. The first with his daughter Krystal at Crufts where he took Best of Breed under judge the late Mr Owen Grindey. He should have won more, but his breeder Mrs Olwyn Harbottle always promised that once he had been beaten by his son Jaspar, she would retire him. Olwyn was true to her word.

Unfortunately no study photographs were ever taken of this lovely mahogany dog in his prime. He was a joy to see in the ring, so sound on the move. His sire was the very glamorous Winterlea Intoo Aes and his dam, the Powderpuff Cresta of Capilon (sister of Clogheen Martello). He has sired 4 UK Champions and to date is still enjoying life with his new owner Mrs Val Blore.

CHAMPION PETWORTH MOPPY TOP

Whelped: 27-9-82
Colour: Blue
Breeder: Mrs M. Hazelman

		Winterlea Intoo Aes	Ming Li of Winterlea
	Ch Aes Into Dynasty		Winterlea Sunbelle
		Cresta of Capilon (Powderpuff)	Staround Quanto
Ch Petworth Moppy Top			Clogheen Natasha
		Demidoff Elvis	Staround Soso of Demidoff
	Petworth China Doll		St Erme Sun Orchid
		Rhodecot Shamsha	Staround Impo
			Staround Calanda

This dark slate-blue bitch was the third Champion sired by Ch Aes Into Dynasty. A lovely size with very glamorous crest and plume. In all, she won twenty-two CCs, dominating the show ring for almost five years. A breed record she held alone until 1990. She now shares it with another Dynasty Champion bitch, Aes Blue Dy-Amond for Movalian. Unfortunately, she never had a litter to carry on the line.

CHAMPION KRYSTAL OF KOJAK (J.W.)

Whelped: 31-7-80
Colour: Blue
Breeders: Mrs OlwynHarbottle
Owners: Mr & Mrs Barrie Jones

		Winterlea Intoo Aes	Ming Li of Winterlea
	Ch Aes Into Dynasty		Winterlea Sunbelle
		Cresta of Capilon (Powderpuff)	Staround Quanto
			Clogheen Natasha
Ch Krystal of Kojak		Sandcrest Aznavour in Blue	Staround Quanto
			Staround Hila
	Pekevista Mei Mei Shan of Aes		Highclass Hairless Blue Boy
		Arrendene Highclass Chinese Moonshine (German import)	Highclass Gypsy Girl

*Champion
Krystal
of Kojak
(J.W.)*

Due to business pressures, her dam Pekevista Mei Mei Shan of Aes was loaned by Mrs Harbottle in the summer/spring of 1980. The resulting litter of six puppies was a great thrill for us to rear. We kept three, Krystal, Jaspar and Sapphire, Olwyn had Diamond, Diadem and Dynamic. Together with her brother Jaspar and sire Dynasty they dominated the show ring in 1982.

Krystal was the first UK bitch Champion, which she achieved on the same day as her sire, under judge Mr Lionel Hamilton-Renwick. She was retired after winning eight CCs and still enjoys a day out at Club shows in the Veteran class. She is a very glamorous, sweet-natured bitch with a mind of her own. She was once featured on television with Barbara Woodhouse.

CHAMPION MOONSWIFT BLUE BARRACUDA

Whelped: 21-5-1983
Colour: Blue
Breeder/Owner: Mrs Diana Bowdler Townsend

			Am. Ch Gipez Ying Ming of Mordor
		Am. Ch Chinacrest Mohawk	
			Zanzibars Terraco
	Am. Ch Razzmatazz Pod		
			Am. Ch Gipez's Wu Ching
Ch Moonswift Blue Barracuda		Am. Ch Gipez's Belle Noire	
			Gipez's Kaity-Tong (Powderpuff)
			Staround Wee Wo
		Cannybuff Cassanova of Moonswift	
	Moonswift Scanlite		Cannybuff Cala
			Staround Romeo
		Saridaks Julietta	
			Heathermount Inza

This blue dog has very interesting breeding. His sire is the American import Am. Ch Razzmatazz Pod and the mating to Moonswift Scanlite has brought forward all the early dogs. It will be interesting to watch the future development from this line.

CHAMPION HANDERBY SNOWQUEEN

Whelped: 31-12-1981
Colour: Blue/pink
Breeder: Mr Ian Richards
Owner: Mrs S. Andrews and Mrs St Erme Cardew

			Staround Koko
		Staround Romeo	
			Staround Hunta
	Carmichan Blue Demon		
			Heathermount Mr Quop
		Carmigan Heavenly Blue	
Ch Handerby Snowqueen			Heathermount Roxanne
			Staround Koko
		Staround Romeo	
			Staround Hunta
	Saridaks Snowflake		
			Cannybuff Cilva
		Heathermount Provacative	
			Winterlea Moon Goddess of Heathermount

This little bitch and her brother Maximillion won many awards. Maximillion won one CC for his owner-breeder, the late Ian Richards who sadly died at a very young age. Snowqueen won twelve Reserve CCs before winning her final qualifying CC, which proves that it is worth persevering.

INTERNATIONAL WORLD CHAMPION: HIGHCLASS MR CHING LEE OF AES

Whelped: January 1976
Colour: Mahogany
Breeder: Herr Alraun
Owner: Mrs Olwyn Harbottle

Int. World Ch. Highclass Mr Ching Lee of Aes
- Int. Ch. Staround Wanto
  - Staround Koko
    - Staround Ahn Ahn Lee
    - Sobesta of Cresthaven
  - Staround Peacha
    - Staround Ahn Ahn Lee
    - Enga of Cresthaven
- El Chiquitins Lotos Blume
  - Bundessg. Me Too of Cresthaven
    - Navo of Cresthaven
    - Byla of Cresthaven
  - Fair Ra of Cresthaven
    - Marbo of Cresthaven
    - Bluga of Cresthaven

This dog was imported by Mrs Olwyn Harbottle. He was already past his prime for the show ring, but he had a great influence in breeding programmes. He was noted for a sound temperament, good feet and ribcage, and level topline.

CHAMPION HEATHERMOUNT PHAROAH OF MOONSWIFT

Whelped: 28-10-1977
Colour: Mahogany
Breeder: Mr F. Parker
Owner: Mrs D. Bowdler-Townsend

Heathermount Pharoah
- Cannybuff Cilva
  - Staround Expo
    - Staround Apollo
    - Staround China Princess
  - Staround Channa
    - Staround Koko
    - Staround Lhaza
- Winterlea Moon Goddess of Heathermount
  - Ming Li of Winterlea
    - Horn of Cresthaven
    - Winterlea Inza of Cresthaven
  - Heathermount Phoenix of Winterlea
    - Staround Quanto
    - Staround Java

This mahogany dog is a good example of the deer type. He has very attractive lacing on his chest. He had great success in the show ring, winning four CCs and Reserve in Group at the Windsor Championship show in 1982. At the time of publication he is still going strong at the grand old age of thirteen years and is much loved by his owner Mrs Diana Bowdler-Townsend.

Champion Jaspar of Kojak

CHAMPION JASPAR OF KOJAK (J.W.)
Whelped: 31-7-1980
Colour: Blue
Breeder: Mrs Olwyn Harbottle
Owner: Mrs Karen Richards

			Ming Li of Winterlea
		Winterlea Intoo Aes	
	Ch. Aes Into Dynasty		Winterlea Sunbelle
			Staround Quanto
		Cresta of Capilon (Powderpuff)	
Ch. Jaspar of Kojak			Clogheen Natasha
			Staround Quanto
		Sandcrest Aznavour in Blue	
	Pekevista Mei Mei Shan of Aes		Staround Hila
			Highclass Hairess Blue Boy
		Arrendene Highclass Chinese Moonshine (German import)	
			Highclass Gypsy Girl

Owned by my daughter Karen Richards, Jaspar gained his title at the end of 1982, and since then he has represented the breed in many books, including The Kennel Club Book of Illustrated Breed Standards. He was finally retired with eight CCs and sired four UK Champions. His photograph was taken when in his prime at three years of age after winning Reserve in Group at the Leeds Championship show, where the judge was The Maharajah of Baria. Jaspar sadly died in 1988 leaving a legacy of good dogs behind him.

CHAMPION MINSKIP GEORGIE OF KHRISJAN
Whelped: 18-11-1982
Colour: Powderpuff, cream
Breeder: Mrs J. Hanna-Turner
Owner: Mr & Miss Donkin

Ch. Minskip Georgie of Khrisjan	Sandcrest Blue Print	Staround Romeo	Staround Koko
			Staround Hunta
		Carmighan Heavenly Blue	Heathermount Mr Quips
			Heathermount Roxanne
	St Erme Blush Orchid	Staround Questo	Staround Kung Foo
			Starbound China Lee
		Clogheen Coleena	Staround Quanto
			Staround Irma

The second Powderpuff male to gain his title, campaigned by his dedicated young owner Christina Donkin and bred by Mrs Jean Hanna-Turner. A very free-moving dog to whom I gave the Reserve CC in 1987.

CHAMPION CLOGHEEN DONNA

Whelped: 3-11-1981
Colour: Blue/pink
Breeder: Mrs Mary Smith
Owner: Mrs Mary Smith

Ch Clogheen Donna			
	Clogheen Martello	Staround Quanto	Staround Koko
			Staround Hunta
		Clogheen Natasha	Staround Quanto
			Staround Irma
	Clogheen Selena	Staround Quanto	Staround Koko
			Staround Hunta
		Clogheen Natasha	Staround Quanto
			Staround Irma

This little bitch added much glamour to the show ring with her flowing crest and plume. She won nine CCs in all and had a very successful career at all levels.

CHAMPION CLOGHEEN PERRY

Whelped: 30-10-1980
Colour: Blue
Breeder: Mrs M. Smith
Owner: Miss J. Gorwill

Ch Clogheen Perry			
	Staround Mordor Anatol	Hey Der of Cresthaven	Alto of Cresthaven
			Fusa of Cresthaven
		Mordor Minnie Pearl	St Jo Battles Muschen
			China Tea Rose
	Clogheen Ann Wong	Staround Ahn Ahn Lee	Lee Chee Lee
			Chi Chi Lee
		Staround Irma	Staround Ahn Ahn Lee
			Staround Danta

This blue dog won just three CCs before being retired. He was sired by Staround Mordor Anatol, an American dog imported by the late Mrs Ruth Harris.

CHAMPION MOONSWIFT MR RAFFLES OF RODRIDGE

Whelped: 27-4-84
Colour: Mahogany
Breeders: Mrs D. Bowdler-Townsend
Owner: Mrs R. Harris

			Staround Ahn Ahn Lee
		Staround Koko	
			Sobesta of Cresthaven
	Staround Romeo		
			Staround Ahn Ahn Lee
		Staround Hunta	
			Staround China Princess
Ch Moonswift Mr			Cannybuff Cilva
Raffles of Rodridge		Ch Heathermount	
		Pharoah of	Winterlea Moon Godess
		Moonswift	of Heathermount
	Moonswift Painted		
	Lily		Staround Romeo
		Saridaks Julietta	
			Heathermount Inza

This dog was originally campaigned by Mr Stuart Smith but he gained his title with the late Mrs Ruth Harris. Sired by the very well known Staround Romeo, for whom CCs arrived too late. Romeo lived to the grand old age of fifteen years, and died in 1990.

CHAMPION CLOGHEEN SADIE

Whelped: 4-7-1982
Colour: Blue
Owner/Breeder: Mrs Mary Smith

This bitch is bred the same way as Ch Clogheen Donna. She was the winner of many top awards.

*Champion
Kojak
Kavalier*

CHAMPION KOJAK KAVALIER

Whelped: 9-4-84
Colour: Blue
Owner/Breeders: Mr & Mrs Barrie Jones

Ch Kojak Kavalier	Ch Jaspar of Kojak	Ch Aes Into Dynasty	Winterlea Into Aes
			Cresta of Capilon (Powderpuff)
		Pekevista Mei Mei Shan of Aes	Sandcrest Aznavour in Blue
			Arrendene Highclass Chinese Moonshine
	Swedish Ch Kojak Kween of the Mei	Ch Jaspar of Kojak	Ch Aes into Dynasty
			Pekevista Mei Mei Shan of Aes
		Aes Mei Ching	Int World Ch Highclass Mr Ching Lee Aes
			Pekevista Mei Mei Shan of Aes

'Fred' as he is known at home is the extrovert of our kennel. Sired by Ch Jaspar of Kojak, he loved every minute in the show ring. To date, he holds the male record of seventeen CCs. His dam Kojak Kween of The Mei won two Reserve CCs before being exported to Lisa Allrin in Sweden where she gained her Swedish title.

*Champion
Aes Blue Dy-
Amond For
Movalian.*

CHAMPION AES BLUE DY-AMOND FOR MOVALIAN

Whelped: 23-11-86
Colour: Blue
Breeder: Mrs Olwyn Harbottle
Owner: Mrs V. Blore

		Winterlea Intoo Aes	Ming Li of Winterlea
	Ch Aes Into Dynasty		Winterlea Sunbelle
		Cresta of Capilon (Powderpuff)	Staround Quanto
Ch Aes Blue Dy-Amond for Moravian			Clogheen Natasha
		Aes Into Horatio	Winterlea Intoo Aes
	Aes September Song		Aes Dy-Adem
		Aes Ka-Milla	Kojak Kharisma of Aes
			Pekevista Mei Mei Shan of Aes

This is the last bitch bred by the late Mrs Olwyn Harbottle, although she was reared and cared for by her owner Mrs Val Blore from just two days old. Sired by Ch Aes Into Dynasty, she has made breed history by being the first Chinese Crested to win a Toy group at a Championship show in Great Britain. The show was Leeds 1988, the judge Mrs Dorothy Dearn. She commands attention in the ring and has to date twenty-two CCs, sharing the breed record with her half-sister Ch Petworth Moppytop.

*Champion
Kojak
Kryspar
(J.W.)*

This handsome son of Ch Jaspar of Kojak has superb conformation and free flowing movement. Owned and campaigned by our daughter Karen Richards, he has won many awards at shows of all levels. He won three CCs before being retired from serious competition.

CHAMPION. KOJAK KRYSPAR (J.W.)
Whelped: 16-4-1984
Colour: Blue
Breeders: Mr & Mrs Barrie Jones
Owners: Mr & Mrs Richards

		Ch Aes Into Dynasy	Winterlea Intoo Aes
	Ch Jaspar of Kojak		Cresta of Capilon (Powerpuff)
		Pekevista Mei Mei Shan of Aes	Sandcrest Aznavour in Blue
Ch Kojak Kryspar			Arrendene Highclass Chinese Moonshine
		Ch Aes Into Dynasty	Winterlea Intoo Aes
	Ch Krystal of Kojak		Cresta of Capilon (Powderpuff)
		Perevista Mei Mei Shan of Aes	Sandcrest Aznavour in Blue
			Arrendene Highclass Chinese Moonshine

CHAMPION MOONSWIFT MR WU OF APOCODEODAR

Whelped: 27-4-84
Colour: Blue
Breeder: Mrs D. Bowdler-Townsend
Owners: Mrs S. Stevenson

		Staround Koko	Staround Ahn Ahn Lee
			Sobesta of Cresthaven
	Staround Romeo		
		Staround Hunta	Staround Ahn Ahn Lee
			Staround China Princess
Ch Moonswift Mr Wu of Apocodeodar			Cannybuff Cilva
		Ch Heathermount Pharoah of Moonswift	Winterlea Moon Goddess of Heathermount
	Moonswift Miss Dixie		
		Moonswift Demelza	Clogheen Martello
			Heathermount Inza

This little dog, bred by Mrs Bowdler-Townsend, was owned and campaigned by the late Sylvia Stevenson who was well known for her Apocodeodar Chihuahua kennel. He was a real showman who retired after winning three CCs.

*Champion
Kojak
Konkorde
(J.W.)*

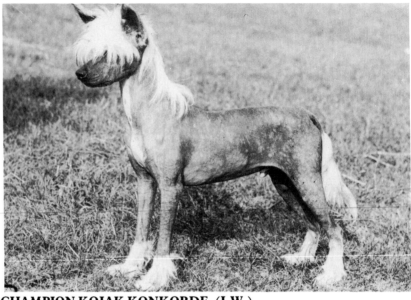

CHAMPION KOJAK KONKORDE. (J.W.)
Whelped: 13-1-84
Colour: Blue
Breeders: Mr & Mrs Barrie Jones
Owners: Mr & Mrs Barrie Jones later Mr & Mrs Jenkins

			Winterlea Intoo Aes
		Ch Aes Into Dynasty	
			Cresta of Capilon (Powderpuff)
	Ch Jaspar of Kojak		
			Sandcrest Aznavour in Blue
		Pekivista Mei Shan of Aes	
			Arrendene Highclass Chinese Moonshine
Ch Kojak Konkorde			
			Int Ch Staround Wanto
		Int World Ch Highclass Mr Ching Lee of Aes	
			El Chiquitins Lotus Blume
	Aes Mei Ching		
			Sandcrest Aznavour in Blue
		Perevista Mei Mei Shan of Aes	
			Arrendene Highclass Chinese Moonshine

A son of Ch Jaspar of Kojak, he was a joy to show, always on his toes like an eager terrier. To be critical of him, I would have liked him a little smaller but he had great ring presence. He won three CCs at consecutive shows. His first as a puppy under the late Bobby James, second at Crufts 1987 under Mr Lionel Hamilton-Renwick and his third from Mr Joe Braddon. He is the grandson of the German import Int. Ch Highclass Mr Ching Lee of Aes. He won a fourth and fifth CC at the age of six years.

CHAMPION KIVOX WREN
(Sandcrest Blue Print – Shan Tung Rialo At Kivox)
Whelped: 12-6-1985
Colour: Black and white Powderpuff
Breeder: Miss I. V. Cox
Owner: Mrs S. Wrenn

*Champion
Kivox
Wren*

A consistent winner of shows of all levels, always immaculately presented by his owner Mrs Sheila Wrenn. Gained his title in 1990.

CHAMPION. DEBRITA DICTATOR

Whelped: 29-9-85
Colour: Blue
Breeder: Mrs T. Dixon

		Dynastie of Debrita	Clogheen Martello
	Debrita Decisive		Heathermount Inza
		Sandcrest Topaz	Staround Romeo
Champion Debrita Dictator			Sandcrest Isa
		Dynastie of Debrita	Clogheen Martello
	Debrita Daisi-Mai		Heathermount Inza
		Welsh Little Star of Sasanataba	Demidoff So Curry
			Demidoff So Candyfloss

This little dog won four CCs in all. His sire Debrita Decisive was unlucky not to gain his title as he won two CCs and was a real little showman.

CHAMPION KOJAK KORONA OF JHANCHI

Whelped: 14-3-1988
Colour: Blue
Breeder: Barrie & Brenda Jones
Owner: Alan & Janet Knowles

		Ch. Kojak Kavalier	Ch. Jaspar of Kojak
	Kojak Kordonbleu		Swedish Ch. Kojak Kween of the Mei
		Kojak Krystina	Ch. Jaspar of Kojak
Ch. Kojak of Jhanchi			Ch. Krystal of Kojak
		Cannybuff Casanova of Moonswift	Staround Wee Woo
	Belmuriz Blueberry of Kojak		Cannybuff Cala
		Winterlea Giselle of Apocodeodar	Ming Li of Winterlea
			Winterlea Sunbelle

A son of Kojak Kordonbleu, 'Badger' is owned by Alan and Janet Knowles and is still enjoying a very successful show career with six CCs to date. His dam Belmuriz Blueberry of Kojak was bred by Mrs Carrie Murrey of the world famous Belmuriz

Chihuahuas. She is a very neat cobby type carrying some of the old bloodlines. Shown very little but won a Reserve CC.

Champion Kojak Kandykisses (J.W.)

CHAMPION. KOJAK KANDYKISSES. (J.W.)
Whelped: 24-7-84
Colour: Blue
Breeders: Mr & Mrs Barrie Jones
Owner: Mr Jim Hall

		Ch Aes Into Dynasty	Winterlea Intoo Aes
	Ch Jaspar of Kojak		Cresta of Capilon (Powderpuff)
		Pekevista Mei Mei Shan of Aes	Sandcrest Aznavour In Blue
Ch Kojak Kandykisses			Arrendene Highclass Chinese Moonshine
		Kojak Kottonsocks	Winterlea Intoo Aes
	Kojak Kottonkandy (Powderpuff)		Cannybuff Christy
		Ch Krystal of Kojak	Ch Aes Into Dynasty
			Cresta of Capilon (Powderpuff)

A daughter of Ch Jaspar of Kojak, Kandy is owned by Mr Jim Hall of the Donsal Salukis. This elegant bitch is renowned for her beautiful free-flowing movement. It is a great joy to see her free running with her Saluki kennelmates, who stand between her and any dog they may meet. She won three CCs before retirement.

CHAMPION THE MASTERBLASTER AT PEKIKI

Whelped: 18-7-1984
Powderpuff: Grey/cream
Breeder: Mr F. Parker
Owner: Mrs M. Godfrey

		Clogheen Martello	Staround Quanto
	Heathermount Victor		Clogheen Natasha
			Staround Mr Wu
		Heathermount Viola	
Ch The Masterblaster At Pekiki			Staround Java
			Staround Wee Wo
		Cannybuff Casanova of Moonswift	
	Cartergate Anna		Cannybuff Cala
			Horn of Cresthaven
		Heathermount Xanadu (Powderpuff)	
			Heathermount Renata

Another little dog who enjoyed showing. A very pretty cream sable bred by Mr Foster Parker of the Heathermount kennel. His dam Cartergate Anna was a very pretty bitch who won many awards before CCs were allocated. He made breed history by becoming the first UK Champion Powderpuff. He had great success at shows of all levels, winning three CCs before retirement.

CHAMPION HEATHERMOUNT IMPERIAL

Whelped: 9-10-1987
Colour: Mahogany
Breeder: F. W. Parker
Owner: Mr Hymes & Mr Parker

			Staround Koko
		Staround Romeo	
			Staround Hunta
	Ch Moonswift Mr Wu of Apocodeodar		
			Ch Heathermount Pharoah of Moonswift
		Moonswift Miss Dixie	
Ch Heathermount Imperial			Moonswift Demelza
			Staround Mr Wu
		Cartergate Beau Jeste	
			Cartergate Ana
	Heathermount Li Chi		
			Ch Aes into Dynasty
		Heathermount Astrid	
			Sahrida of Heathermount

This mahogany dog was bred by Mr Foster Parker and jointly owned with Mr Tony Hynes. A dog with a very nice head and winner of four CCs.

CHAMPION PEANDOKRY SALLY OF CLOGHEEN

Whelped: 8-10-1987
Colour: Blue/pink
Breeder: Mr A. Rachael
Owner: Mrs M. Smith

			Dynastie of Debrita
		Debrita Decisive	
			Sandcrest Topza
	Debrita Dexter		
			Dynastie of Debrita
		Debrita Delicate Jade	
Ch Peandokry Sally of Clogheen			Superlion Simply Exquisite of Peandokry
			Staround Romeo
		Rodridge Ricardo of Clogheen	
			Moonswift Pussy Galore
	Pendokry Dylans Desire		
			Sobahn Sebastion at Superlion
		Superlion Simply Exquisite of Peanokry	
			Ge-Joel Phoenix Rose of Denroma

Winner of three CCs to date, and still active in the show ring.

CHAMPION DEBRITA DEVIL IN DISGUISE

Whelped: 6-6-1985
Colour: Cream powderpuff
Owner/Breeder: Mrs T. Dixon

Ch Debrita Devil in Disguise	Debrita Decisive	Dynastie of Debrita	Clogheen Martello
			Heathermount Inza
		Sandcrest Topaz	Staround Romeo
			Sandcrest Isa
	Superlion Snowflake	Sobahn Sebastian at Superlion	Sobahn Sedaka
			Sobahn Blachette
		Welsh Little Star of Sasanataba	Demidoff So Curry
			Quipp of Demidoff

The first and to date the only bitch Champion Powderpuff. I awarded her a Reserve CC in 1987. A year later my husband Barrie gave her the CC, which was the first to be won by a bitch Powderpuff. A very full-coated cream, always handled by Dawn Dixon for her mother.

CHAMPION TOTSDOWN TRIXIE OF FREELANE

Whelped: 28-11-1987
Colour: Blue
Breeder: Mr & Mrs Wheeler
Owner: Mrs & Miss Gorwill

Ch Totsdown Trixie of Freelane	Alltot Tai Shan	Staround Millers Raven of Allegazoo Rivercrest
		Alltot Mei Lou
	Alltot Cinderella	Ch Clogheen Perry
		Jefalfy Chrysanthemum

A very pretty bitch of lovely type. To date she has three CCs, her first gained at the tender age of just six months.

CHAMPION KOJAK KAVALKADE
Whelped: 12-10-85
Colour: Blue
Breeders/owners: Mr & Mrs Barrie Jones

			Ch Aes into Dynasty
		Ch Jaspar of Kojak	
			Pekevista Mei Mei Shan of Aes
	Ch Kojak Kavalier		
			Ch Jaspar of Kojak
		Swedish Ch Kojak Kween of The Mei	Aes Mei Ching
Ch Kojak Kavalkade			
			Winterlea Intoo Aes
		Kojak Kottonsocks	
			Cannybuff Christy
	Kojak Kottonkandy		
			Ch Aes Into Dynasty
		Ch Krystal of Kojak	
			Pekevista Mei Mei Shan of Aes

Daughter of Ch Kojak Kavalier and a Powderpuff daughter of Ch Krystal of Kojak. At six months old she was awarded Best in Show at an Open show under Mr Harry Jordan and fulfilled this promise with four CCs and many other awards before retirement.

*Champion
Itzcuintli
Xquisite*

CHAMPION ITZCUINTLI XQUISITE
Whelped: 14-11-1988
Colour: Blue
Breeder: Mike & Karen Richards
Owner: Mike & Karen Richards

			Ch Jaspar of Kojak
		Ch Kojak Kavalier	
	Kojak Kordonbleu		Swedish Ch Kojak Kween of the Mei
			Ch Jaspar of Kojak
		Kojak Krystina	
Ch Itzcuintli Xquisite			Ch Krystal of Kojak
			Ch Jaspar of Kojak
		Ch Kojak Kavalier	
	Kojak Kalypso		Swedish Ch Kojak Kween of the Mei
			Pekevista Fu Hsi Chan
		Pekevista Sum Chik Mei of Kojak	
			Arrendene Highclass Chinese Moonshine

This beautiful young bitch gained her title in 1990. She won
many awards as a puppy and her early promise has been fulfilled
with three CCs to date. Her sire, Kojak Kordonbleu, has sired
two UK champions, but he dislikes the show ring himself.
Xquisite's dam won two Reserve CCs before having to be retired
after breaking a leg.

AMERICAN

*American
Champion
Razzmatazz
Snapdragon*

AMERICAN CHAMPION RAZZMATAZZ SNAPDRAGON

Am. Ch Razzmatazz Snapdragon	Ch China Crest Mohawk	Ch Gipez Ying-Ming of Mordor	Tod-Mar's Double Trouble
			Mordor Melissa Rose
		Zanaibar's Terraco	Phaedrian's Spooky Devil Dog
			Tiny Tia of Fawn Crest
	Ch Gipez Belle Noire	Ch Gipez Hu-Ching	Ch Gipez Ying-Ming of Mordor
			Ch Mordor Marina of Gipez
		Gipez Kaity-Tong	Ch Phaedrian's Key-Ling of Rivercrest
			Gipez Lou-Chow

Bred by Amy Fernandez, this bitch is sister to the UK import Ch Razzmatazz Pod. She is the winner of many top awards including: Best of Winners at the 1986 ACCC National under Mrs Bowdler-Townsend. She finished with all Majors and a multiple Best of Breed and Group winner. She is a very nice type with classic markings and correct feet. Mated to Am. Ch Kojak King of The Blues she produced Ch Razzmatazz Formal Attire and her sister Ch Razzmatazz Wild Wings.

AMERICAN CHAMPION RAZZMATAZZ JUBILATION
Whelped: 1-3-1988

			Ch Jaspar of Kojak
		Ch Kojak Kavalier	
			Kojak Kween of the Mei
	Ch Kojak King of the Blues		
			Ch Jaspar of Kojak
		Kojak Krystina	
			Ch Krystal of Kojak
Am. Ch Razzmatazz Jubilation			
			Ch Gipez Ying-Ming of Mordor
		Ch China Crest Mohawk	
			Zanzibar's Terraco
	Ch Razzmatazz Dragonfly		
			Ch Gipez Hu-Ching
		Ch Gipez Belle Noire	
			Gipez Kaity-Tong

A son of Am. Ch Kojak King of The Blues and Am. Ch Razzmatazz Dragonfly, and winner of many awards. This mating has brought out the best of both blood lines.

American Champion China Crest Mohawk

AMERICAN CHAMPION CHINA CREST MOHAWK
Whelped: 26-4-1983

			Mordor L'Ono
		Tod-Mar's Double Trouble of Mordor	
	Ch Gipez's Ying-Ming of Mordor		Lucky Crest's Huni Lotus of Rivercrest
			Mordor L'ono
		Mordor Melissa Rose	
Am. Ch China Crest Mohawk			Mordor Minnie Pearl
			Ch Phaedrian's Key-Ling of Rivercrest
		Phaedrian's Spooky Devil Dog	
	Zanzibar's Terraco		Phaedrian's Mira'ca of Crest Haven
			Prator's War Lord
		Tiny Tia of Fawn Crest	
			Prator's Ms China Mint

This dog was bred by Mr Paul Ancil in 1983 and is the top sire in the USA having produced twenty-three Champions and four European and International Champions. Not heavily crested, he has lovely skin and long hare feet. His head is very well balanced with a strong underjaw.

*American
Champion
Razzmatazz
Peppermint
Twist.*

AMERICAN CHAMPION RAZZMATAZZ PEPPERMINT TWIST
Whelped: 1-10-87

			Ch Jaspar of Kojak
		Ch Kojak Kavalier	
			Kojak Kween of the Mei
	Ch Kojak King of the Blues		
			Ch Jaspar of Kojak
		Kojak Krystina	
			Ch Krystal of Kojak
Am Ch Razzmatazz Peppermint Twist			
			Ch Gipez Ying-Ming of Mordor
		Ch Gipez Hu-Ching	
			Ch Mordor Marina of Gipez
	Ch Gipez Belle Noir		
			Ch Phaedrian's Key-Ling of Rivercrest
		Gipez Kaity-Tong	
			Gipez Lou-Chow

This dog is the result of one of the first matings of the dog imported from the US by Amy Fernandez. It is interesting to see how the head type has carried through and the strong quarters. Peppermint Twist is a multiple speciality and All Breed Best in Show winner. To date he is the sire of six Champions.

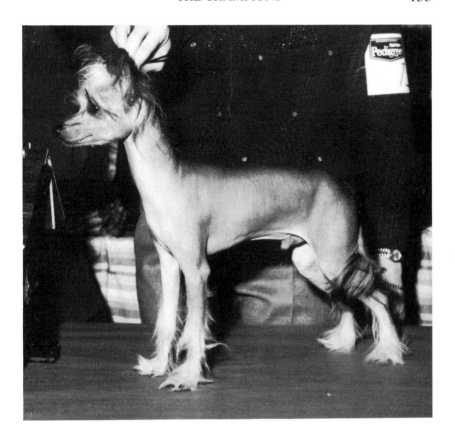

AMERICAN CHAMPION RAZZMATAZZ FORMAL ATTIRE
Whelped: 7-21-88

			Ch Jaspar of Kojak
		Ch Kojak Kavalier	
			Kojak Kween of the Mei
	Ch Kojak King of the Blues		
			Ch Jaspar of Kojak
		Kojak Krystina	
			Ch Krystal of Kojak
Am Ch Razzmatazz Formal Attire			
			Ch Gipez Ying-Ming of Mordor
		Ch China Crest Mohawk	
			Zanzibar's Terraco
	Ch Razzmatazz Snapdragon		
			Ch Gipez Hu-Ching
		Ch Gipez Belle Noire	
			Gipez Kaity-Tong

AMERICAN CHAMPION RAZZMATAZZ DRAGONFLY

Am. Ch Razzmatazz Dragonfly	Ch China Crest Mohawk	Ch Gipez Ying-Ming of Mordor	Tod-Mar's Double Trouble
			Mordor Melissa Rose
		Zanzibar's Terraco	Phaedrian's Spooky Devil Dog
			Tiny Tia of Fawn Crest
	Ch Gipez Belle Noire	Ch Gipez Hu-Ching	Ch Gipez Ying-Ming of Mordor
			Ch Mordor Marina of Gipez
		Gipez Kaity-Tong	Ch Phaedrian's Key-Long of Rivercrest
			Gipez Lou-Chow

AMERICAN CHAMPION LEJO'S HALO OF PHAEDRIAN
Whelped: 16-12-82

Am Ch Lejo's Halo of Phaedrian	Ch Phaedrian's Keyling of Rivercrest	Lou-Ell's Choy Ling of Rivercrest	
		China Key of Rivercrest	
	Ch Chantilly Phaedrian	Ch Phaedrian's Key Ling of Rivercrest	
		Ch Harvest Phaedrian	

The Phaedrian Kennel of Hazel Willard has produced many Champions. Ch Lejo's Halo of Phaedrian owned by Lee and John Bakuckas was one of the top bitches in America before her retirement. She is the dam of multiple BIS winner Ch Lejo's Vladimir, Ch Lejo's Pegasus and Ch Lejo's Pandora.

American Champion Kojak King of the Blues

AMERICAN CHAMPION KOJAK KING OF THE BLUES

			Ch Aes into Dynasty
		Ch Jaspar of Kojak	
			Pekevista Mei Mei Shan of Aes
	Ch Kojak Kavalier		
			Ch Jaspar of Kojak
		Kojak Kween of the Mei	
			Ch Aes Mei-Ching
Am Ch Kojak King of the Blues			Ch Aes Into Dynasty
		Ch Jaspar of Kojak	
			Pekevista Mei Mei Shan of Aes
	Kojak Krystina		
			Ch Aes Into Dynasty
		Ch Krystal of Kojak	
			Pekevista Mei Mei Shan of Aes

'Basil' has fulfilled all expectations. He was imported to combine his qualities with those of the Razzmattaz Kennel and has proved a great success. To date he has sired ten American and three European Champions.

American Champion Razzmatazz Wild Wings.

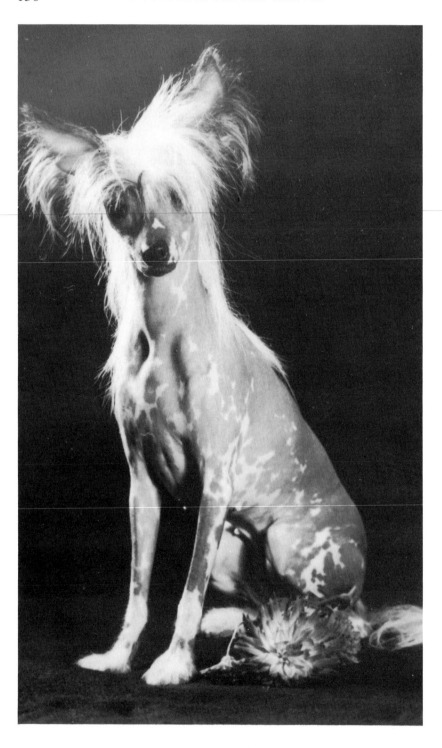

AMERICAN CHAMPION. RAZZMATAZZ WILD WINGS
Whelped: 21-7-88

			Ch Jaspar of Kojak
		Ch Kojak Kavalier	
			Kojak Kween of the Mei
	Ch Kojak King of the Blues		
			Ch Jaspar of Kojak
		Kojak Krystina	
			Ch Krystal of Kojak
Am Ch Razzmatazz Wild Wings			
			Ch Gipez Ying-Ming of Mordor
		Ch China Crest Mohawk	
			Zanzibar's Terraco
	Ch Razzmatazz Snapdragon		
			Ch Gipez Hu-Ching
		Ch Gipez Belle Noire	
			Gipez Kaity-Tong

American Champion Razzmatazzmanian Devil.

AMERICAN CHAMPION RAZZMATAZZMANIAN DEVIL

Am. Ch Razzmatazzmanian Devil			
	Ch China Crest Mohawk	Ch Gipez Ying-Ming of Mordor	Tod Mar's Double Trouble P.P.
			Mordor Melissa Rose H.L.
		Zanzibar's Terraco H.L	Phaedrian's Spooky Devil Dog H.L.
			Tiny Tia of Fawn Crest H.L.
	Ch Gipez's Belle Noire	Ch Gipez's Hu-Ching H.L.	Ch Gipez's Ying-Ming of Mordor H.L.
			Ch Mordor Marina of Gipez P.P.
		Gipez's Kaity-Tong P.P.	Ch Phaedrians Key-Ling of Rivercrest
			Gipez Lou-Chow P.P.

APPENDIX

BREED CLUBS

The Chinese Crested Club Of Great Britain,
Mrs Brenda Taylor,
8 High Street,
Stilton,
Peterborough,
Cambridgeshire,
Great Britain.

The Chinese Crested Dog Club,
Mr Arthur Broadhead,
The Gorge,
83 Gorge Road,
Coseley,
Bilston,
Wolverhampton,
West Midlands,
Great Britain.

The American Chinese Crested Club,
Mr Dick Dickerson,
2706 Murfreeboro Pike,
Nashville,
TN 37013,
U. S. A.

The American Hairless Dog Club,
Box 24 Thompson Bridge Road,
Jackson,
NK. NJ 08527,
U. S. A.

The Xoloitzcuintli Club Of America,
Patricia Weissleader,
71455 18th Avenue,
Desert Hot Springs,
CA 92240,
U. S. A.